Was It Even Abuse?

Restoring clarity after covert abuse

Emma Rose Byham

ISBN: 978-1-7391026-0-9

Dedicated to my family.
Thank you for being my sunshine through the storm.
Especially my hoglets.

Contents

Introduction:

Restoring Clarity

Have you endlessly searched online trying to make sense of their behaviour? *Hoping to understand how they treat you.* Is it normal? Why does it hurt so much? Or perhaps you feel conflicted because you think their behaviour is unacceptable, but you question your ability to judge what acceptable is.

Is it me?

Am I too sensitive?

Am I crazy?

The confusion that engulfs an abusive relationship is mentally exhausting and a major factor to feeling stuck. It is through gaining clarity of your experiences you lay the foundations of a strong and sturdy recovery. You can then shift towards planting seeds of growth. Seeds such as understanding, self-acceptance, self-compassion and validation.

In my opinion, it is essential, because you need to understand what you have been through to process it effectively. We connect everything to this understanding. If you have clarity of your experiences, you can understand the responses you had. When you understand your responses, you can accept them and afford yourself compassion. With clarity, there also comes validation. It is not me. I am not too sensitive. I am not crazy. And, through the power of validation, you open the door to accepting what you've been through. It is with acceptance of ourselves and our experiences we heal.

Clarity is the beginning of building a strong internal world.

I have dedicated my professional and personal development to understanding abusive relationships. To facilitate healing and build awareness of covert abuse. I have studied psychology and counselling and attended courses to get beneath the abusive dynamic. In 2017, I began advocating and have since established an online community to support, validate and raise awareness for survivors of emotional and psychological abuse. It is through this online community and my work that I came to realise the significant effect of post-abuse confusion. It is self-perpetuating, confusion feeding into confusion, spiralling into greater self-doubt and further distress.

The more survivors shared their experiences with me, the more it became clear there are common hurdles to overcome. These centre on how confusion affects our ability to understand and process abusive experiences. Feelings of shame about our own behaviour and the relationship itself. Whether the connection was genuine, and how to break the attachment and feelings of regret. Perhaps most poignantly, the lack of validation when confusion engulfs us.

The overwhelming lack of clarity heavily affects the ability to heal after abuse.

I know the value of restoring clarity, the importance of validation, and how three simple things can bring calmness to your inner turmoil: feeling heard, feeling understood, and feeling believed. Whilst one book cannot capture the nuances of every abusive relationship, this book intends to guide you through the confusion, to support you in restoring clarity and meeting those needs.

Let us take this opportunity to compare post-abuse confusion to watching a foreign language film. You are watching with no subtitles, and you haven't read a plotline. When the film ends, you think you know what it was about, but you feel uncertain. You may feel you have a general overview, but because you didn't understand the language, you question your understanding of the storyline... maybe you misunderstood the meaning of certain parts or perhaps it meant something else entirely.

The first port of call is to read a plotline. Here, you gain clarity. Now you feel you've got a good understanding of the film. Then you read a plotline from a different source, a film synopsis, and an overview too. The more voices you hear on the storyline, the clearer your understanding of it. You build confidence that you have a good grasp of the film's content and its meaning. This is how it feels when you first educate yourself on abusive relationships. The knowledge you gain helps you to understand and make sense of your experiences that have been shrouded in uncertainty. It may feel like a slow awareness running through your veins. Or it may be a sudden realisation.

So how about reading a couple of film reviews for good measure? Here, you start to apply your knowledge and form your own opinion. There are reviews you agree with, and others feel slightly off the mark. Some reviews pick up on aspects of the film you hadn't considered, and this brings a whole other dimension to the storyline. Your understanding grows further. Beforehand, you would have had to consider all reviews (or everyone's opinion of your experiences) equally. With deeper clarity and confidence in your understanding, however, you can trust in your own perception and say, 'this doesn't apply to how I understand my experiences', or 'this deepens my understanding and supports my growth'.

The more knowledge you gain, the more your confidence grows in how well you have understood the film. This means you are less and less reliant on other people's opinions because you now trust your own judgement. You have formed your own opinion based on the clarity you have gained. You no longer question yourself because you have developed your understanding, not through watching the film but through the experience of watching the film and applying the knowledge of the storyline, which you have gained after having watched it.

Growth through clarity of abuse is the same principle; you experience growth as you become clearer in your view of the abuse you were subjected to. The level of self-doubt and confusion shifts because you have an understanding through the experience of abuse, as well as applying the knowledge you gain about abusive relationships to your own experiences. This is why clarity is so important. If you clearly understand the relationship, it validates how you perceive your experiences and allows you to build trust in your truth.

In this book, we will explore four areas that are rife with confusion. I encourage you to write through these pages as moments of clarity emerge. Journalling helps you in having clear thoughts. It also supports you in becoming aware of your emotions and accepting them. This in turn, will reduce stress. I have included prompts, reflections, and affirmations to support you in the process.

The four areas are:

The Three A's: increasing *awareness* of abuse in relationships, to support you in *acknowledging* and *accepting* your own experiences.

Untangling Self: identifying abusive behaviour, trauma responses, and the abusive dynamic to facilitate self-compassion for how you reacted to or have been affected by abuse.

Potential versus Reality: merging the understanding of who the abuser is with the reality to reduce inner conflict and lead towards inner peace.

Breaking the Chains: reframing core beliefs about relationships that keep you tied to the abuser, supporting you in shifting focus onto growth.

There are questions upon questions regarding these four areas. Confusion over what abuse feels like, what counts as abuse, your own behaviour, and how you still react. The distress felt by knowing they mistreated you, yet still feeling a deep longing to be with them or the uncertainty about your decision to leave and your judgement of their character.

Do not underestimate the importance of finding answers to these questions, as they provide a feeling of safety - that you are understood, that you are not alone, and that you are believed. It empowers you to direct your own growth and healing. *You are not crazy.* That you can trust yourself. It builds evidence the toxic messages internalised during abusive relationships that lead to self-doubt, self-blame and worthlessness are exactly that: toxic. Not truth. You can become 'unstuck' and make sense of it all.

Part One

The Three A's

At some point during or after experiencing abuse, there is an awakening. For some survivors, it feels like a catastrophic event, when everything seems to implode or explode or descend into chaos with high levels of distress. For others, it is a slow burning realisation that your experiences were not 'just normal' or how all relationships are, and these experiences directly connect to your own inner struggles and trauma. Some have described it as finally being able to exhale, while others have said it feels like an empty void. No matter how it comes about, the awakening feels unstable. It is shaking up what we think we know; what we think we understand about our world and ourselves and, therefore, our sense of stability.

The three A's are how you first regain stability. These are: Awareness, Acknowledgement and Acceptance.

Awareness is when you gain knowledge about abusive relationships in an impersonal way. Awareness is first developed through understanding the basic principles of abuse, or, as I like to call them, the fundamentals. Clarity of these aspects helps to raise awareness of when it is an abusive relationship dynamic. This is crucial for growth because you become aware not all relationships follow this dynamic. Prior to having a conscious understanding of the fundamentals, you may assume that which you have experienced is part of 'normal' relationship highs and lows. You might feel morally compelled to accept the abuser's poor behaviour for several reasons, such as you believe you should love them unconditionally or you feel responsible for their abusive outbursts. However, this will leave you failing to grasp why it has had such a significant impact on your wellbeing.

Acknowledgement is when you take the knowledge you have gained and apply it to your personal experiences. Once you have developed your awareness of abuse within a relationship objectively, you can begin to acknowledge abusive behaviours and patterns in your own relationship. So, awareness facilitates acknowledgement.

Sometimes, awareness and acknowledgement happen simultaneously, and you literally feel as though you're reading a script from your life. Other times, it takes a little longer for us to recognise the abuse present in our relationships.

The more knowledge you gain, the greater your realisation and understanding of your personal experiences, and this leads to acceptance that there was abuse in the relationship. This stage of acceptance is based on recognising the relationship was abusive and understanding why and how it affected you. It is difficult to accept your intense emotions if you are unaware of the abusive dynamic. This can add to the shame, pain, and instability of the experience. The realisation it was abuse not only validates your pain, it also empowers you, through enabling you to accept the impact it has had.

You equip yourself with the knowledge their behaviour was unacceptable, and a healthy relationship does not involve such mistreatment. It is with acceptance you can rebuild the image of your world and yourself; what you have been through and where you are now. You can integrate your newfound understanding of abusive experiences, providing you again with a feeling of stability.

We can address core questions survivors have through the three A's. In building awareness, acknowledgement, and acceptance, we can gain clarity on:

- Was my relationship abusive?
- Why didn't I just leave?
- Do they do it on purpose?
- Am I the abusive one?
- Am I overreacting?

The confusion and doubt these questions create are closely associated with feelings of fear, shame and guilt. We fear whether we are to blame for the abuse. We doubt whether our emotions and pain are valid and we feel guilty over the way we responded. In gaining a greater understanding of how abusive relationships work, we can answer these questions, we can reduce the feelings of fear and shame that are attached to them and increase our sense of inner peace.

So, the clarity which you gain in the three A's provides you with the initial overview of abusive experiences. It is the wave of understanding when you read the plotline for the first time. The relief of finally making sense of a complex relationship that is riddled with confusion. It is the introduction of a healthier narrative, after being subjected to the abusive one. It is the start of laying stable new foundations.

When you acknowledge the abuse, you can accept the depth of your response. It is proportionate; it is valid.

Chapter one:

Awareness

There are preconceptions about abusers and abusive relationships. For example, the stereotype of a lower class, lower educated male, who is aggressive in his temperament and rough in his nature. We may think, 'if he ever hit me, I would walk out the door'. So, the first unacceptable abuse we have identified is physical. What about the abuse that precedes this? What about the fact that the profile of a lower class, lower educated male can also describe a loving father and husband who is nurturing and a steady provider?

Abusers fit many profiles, but when your own experiences don't match your preconceptions about abuse, it hinders you from understanding and healing from them. When you have a fixed idea of abusive relationships or abusers, which you cannot relate to even though you have been abused, you feel confused and unable to understand what you have experienced. Yet you still feel the impact of abuse. This is a significant cause of distress and leads to a feeling of instability.

Awareness is learning key information about how an abusive relationship actually looks and feels, so you can come away from the stereotypes and lead the way to recognising abuse in your personal experiences.

Question: Was My Relationship Abusive?

First, if you are even asking this question, ask yourself why. Would you be asking this question in a healthy relationship? Would you be doing late night internet searches trying to either self-soothe, validate or make sense of their behaviour? If you are asking this question, your intuition is telling you something is not right.

A common inner struggle with abusive relationships is that you have learned not to trust, or perhaps even hear, your intuition. There are high levels of self-doubt which are part of the abuse, so you no longer trust your gut feeling. It also feels less scary to rationalise and avoid acknowledging the extent of their behaviour than face up to it and what it means. This is totally understandable. With acceptance that it is abuse comes an inevitable transition, and with any transition, there is loss. In an abusive relationship, when everything can be so volatile, we cling onto the current situation for a sense of stability and to avoid experiencing any more loss or pain than we are already experiencing.

Yet, this adds to your confusion.

The lack of clarity over whether the relationship is abusive also causes pain and distress. So, let's break down some key features to answer the question: what is an abusive relationship?

Emotional and Psychological Abuse

An abuser by definition is someone who treats another with cruelty or violence, especially regularly or repeatedly. Whilst this reduces it to its simplest terms and doesn't delve into the complexities of human nature or the reasons abusive patterns develop, it does recognise they are someone who recurringly treats another with callousness. To extend this definition, an abuser is someone who repeatedly seeks control in the power dynamic of intimate relationships. Therefore, I will refer to the person who caused harm throughout this book as an abuser. It is not to reduce them to their negative behaviours or always assume the worst in them. It is, however, to recognise the repeated cruelty of their behaviour, the impact it has, and the power imbalance.

We often use the terms emotional and psychological abuse interchangeably because many abuse tactics have a negative effect on both emotional and psychological wellbeing. But there is a slight difference.

Emotional abuse teaches you that your feelings are wrong. That you should be ashamed of your emotional responses, and you should feel differently. It involves manipulating the way you feel and using your feelings to control you. Emotional abusers target your self-esteem, undermine and invalidate your feelings, shame and blame your emotional reactions, withhold affection, and use coercive control. Coercive control is a pattern of intimidation or humiliation to shame or scare you, to regulate your behaviour.

Psychological abuse teaches you that your perception is wrong. That you cannot trust the way you perceive, and you should think differently. It involves distorting your reality, manipulating the way you think, and using this to control you. Psychological abusers target your trust in your mental capacity, convince you that you're crazy, manipulate your judgement, foster intense levels of self-doubt and use coercive control.

Emotional abuse targets the way you feel, psychological abuse targets the way you think. Both cause significant harm to your mental wellbeing and are difficult to identify within the relationship. For this reason, they are also described as covert abuse.

Patterns

When reflecting on the abusive relationship, gradually what emerges is a consistent pattern of abusive behaviour. Examples of this are consistent put downs, criticism, or insults which create a tapestry of abuse. Emotional and psychological abuse within relationships is highly unlikely to be a single behaviour. I have never heard of it. Although, I would argue, if the abuser did this consistently and with the power imbalance of abuse, it would still have a significant impact.

Usually, however, abuse is interweaving patterns of behaviour that target your self-esteem, independence and ability to trust your own judgement. These patterns operate on micro and macro levels, as well as covert and overt. Not all abusive relationships are identical, and so the combination or variation of these patterns differ. For example, you may have experienced a singular stronger pattern of abusive behaviour with some weaker underlying patterns, or you may have experienced multiple persistent intricate patterns of abuse.

Either way, the result is a blanket undertone of abuse in the relationship.

Micro Patterns

Micro patterns are persistent and frequent patterns of abuse. They often happen on a daily or weekly basis and underpin a substantial amount of communication. Generally, because of the higher frequency of micro patterns, these are covert behaviours, as they rely on subtlety to fly under the radar.

Examples of micro patterns are continuous criticism, snide comments, or jokes at your expense. The abuser shows a general disrespect in their communication towards you. Their go to response is to put you down rather than show appreciation. Or there is a pattern of criticising you when you make an effort, demeaning you when you've had a good day, and dismissing your attempts to share good news. These micro patterns attack your self-esteem and feeling of worth. They invalidate your viewpoint, your feelings and your experiences and create a power imbalance, but on a very low level that is difficult to detect.

As well as patterns that attack your self-esteem, there are micro patterns that attack your sense of reality. These are patterns of blame, minimising and manipulation. The abuser uses guilt when they put you down or blame when they criticise you. Or there is a pattern of minimising or denying when you try to discuss their abusive behaviour, with them claiming it's all in your head.

These micro patterns can cause significant psychological deterioration. In his book, Why Does He Do That?, Lundy Bancroft profiles this type of abuse as a Water Torturer, with a drip, drip, drip, of extremely low level covert abusive behaviour. The behaviour itself may not seem significantly bad, however it becomes abusive through its persistency, callousness, and the inability to avoid it. It feels impossible to gain a sense of stability, as, although the behaviour is felt it is hard to detect, and it is unpredictable as to when and how frequently it will occur, leading to anxiety and furthering mental decline. The action itself may seem minor but through this combination of factors it becomes significant abuse, having a substantial impact on your mental wellbeing.

In an abusive relationship, there might be dozens of tiny but significant patterns of abusive behaviour. It creates the feeling you can never seem to get it right, but you don't know what it is you're doing wrong. This is more dangerous than it may first sound. It can lead you to believe, if you cannot put your finger on what it is *you are doing wrong*, then it must be something that is *inherently wrong with you*.

Macro Patterns

Macro patterns are consistent, albeit less frequent, patterns of abuse. Unlike micro patterns, which can happen on a weekly basis or up to multiple times a day, macro patterns take place over a larger stretch of time. As the frequency is less, there is also the possibility of more overt displays of abuse. Some abusers, however, only ever display covert behaviours and will therefore still abuse covertly during macro patterns. This comprises a rise and fall in the intensity of the micro patterns of abusive behaviour, such as intensified criticism, belittling, or indifference.

Two examples of abusive macro patterns are the explosive rage and ignoring you as punishment, also known as the silent treatment. More overt forms of verbal abuse would also fall into macro patterns, such as yelling, swearing or verbal intimidation. If you log how frequently these behaviours occur, there is likely to be a pattern in their frequency as well. This is because patterns of abuse are entirely to do with the abuser's internal world, and they are likely to repeat the same (inner) process over similar durations of time.

You are not the cause of their abusive behaviour.

There are also macro patterns of creating dysfunction around special occasions, such as birthdays, work promotions or holiday seasons. Special occasions are a time where morale is boosted, and we feel good about ourselves, however, abuse works by keeping morale low, and by keeping your focus on the needs of the abuser. The abuser therefore feels threatened by the shift in the relationship dynamic which occurs at special occasions and responds by amplifying the abuse to regain your full attention, keep self-esteem low, create chaos and maintain control.

This includes orchestrating a huge fight just before the event, so you feel inner turmoil rather than being able to enjoy the celebration. They may also become agitated and accuse you of being self-centred or arrogant if you take pride in an achievement, covertly reminding you that you don't deserve to feel pride in yourself. Or they behave in such a way, others feel uncomfortable and leave early. The abuser might completely ignore the fact it is your birthday, which negatively impacts on self-worth. Or if they acknowledge it, they become upset and accuse you of being ungrateful for their efforts, shifting your focus onto reassuring them to avoid an escalation of abusive behaviour.

These are just some ways the abuser creates dysfunction on special occasions.

Macro patterns build anxiety, anticipation and instil fear. They act as the 'main event' to the micro patterns. The micro patterns are a constant reminder that if you upset the abuser, things could tip over to a macro incident of abuse. We do anything we can to avoid this from happening. When we experience the macro incident, it signals to us that this is a genuine threat and something we want to avoid repeating at all costs. It shifts your focus onto the abuser's needs with even greater vigilance… forgoing your own.

Blanket of Pressure

The interweaving patterns of abuse create a blanket of pressure. There may be weekly patterns of covert abuse, monthly patterns of intensified verbal abuse, half yearly patterns of overt outbursts of abuse and annual patterns of abuse around special occasions. Not all abusive relationships will follow this exact outline, but they incorporate the same principle of interlocking patterns of abusive behaviour, where abuse is an ever-present fixture in the relationship, although not always apparent.

This leads to a significant power imbalance in the relationship.

It is important to recognise abuse as a pattern. It is not simply they are sometimes abusive, but the rest of the time you feel freedom to express yourself. The relationship is never free from the effects of abuse. There are good times, but even during these times, there is a subconscious anticipation of when subtle abuse will re-emerge and lead towards escalated incidents. There is a feeling of walking on eggshells as you don't want to upset the abuser because, in some form, there is always a pattern of abuse underlying in the relationship. Awareness of the abusive undertone provides clarity to the constant feeling of pressure and the question: was my relationship abusive? Even if it isn't always obvious, the effects are always present.

Single Incident Dilemma

People will look for you to explain how abuse was present in the relationship. Often, we ourselves are looking for clear incidents to pinpoint as abusive, to make sense of the relationship. The issue, however, is if you take a single incident of emotional or psychological abuse, or even a single pattern, it loses a significant depth of context. Take, for example, the constant criticisms. If the abuser's criticism over every little thing is most clear in your mind, this is what you explain as their abusive behaviour. However, without knowing the intricacies of the relationship, it is difficult to grasp the severity of abuse from the example of constant criticism. What people may assume is the relationship is the same as many healthier relationships, with the addition of more criticism. This could not be further from reality.

It's a little like reading a single page of a book. You receive a snapshot of information, but without reading the rest of the book, it is difficult to put that one page into the context of its importance or meaning to the book's overall themes and narrative. Pulling out single incidents is the same. A single incident of covert abuse rarely provides a realistic portrayal of the severity of abuse in the relationship, but it is often what we or others depend on to decide the level of abuse that occurred.

5 reflective questions if you feel you are in an abusive relationship:

o   Do they engage in behaviour that consistently puts you down, criticises you, mocks or accuses you, undermines your feelings or that doesn't respect your space, privacy or belongings?

o   Do they use pressure tactics such as sulking, withholding affection, becoming dismissive towards you, withholding access to money, your phone or other people, or using guilt until you change your mind?

o   When you bring up their behaviour, do they deny it, blame you or twist your words, leaving you feeling unsettled about your own perception or feeling crazy?

o   Do you frequently feel on edge or tense around them because of fear of upsetting them?

o   Do you wonder if you are oversensitive, or do they say you're overreacting because it 'wasn't a big deal' or 'was only a joke'?

Question: Why Didn't I Leave?

The question of why a survivor didn't leave sooner shows a basic misunderstanding of the purpose of abuse. The abuse is not intended to push you away; it is used to force you into an environment where you have to stay. Whether that be through mental, emotional, social, financial, or even physical imprisonment.

When we consider the hierarchy of reasons why survivors don't leave an abusive relationship, the very first barriers to overcome are the practical, economical, and social restraints. For example, if you are emotionally ready to leave but don't have the financial means or access to social support, it won't be possible. The abuser makes it exceptionally difficult to leave by cutting off these essential 'escape routes', which is achieved through the cornerstones of abuse. The cornerstones are four aspects that are built upon in an abusive relationship to achieve and maintain the power imbalance and build the walls that keep you trapped, which are:

- Dependency
- Confusion
- Punishment
- Control

An abuser doesn't want you to leave. That would be the ultimate loss of power. If the relationship is to end, they want it to be on their terms.

Isolation (Dependency)

Isolation works like this: through manipulation, such as guilt, shame, veiled threats (fear), or gaslighting, there is a loss of connection with others. As there is no longer connection to others, you form a dependency on the abuser to meet all your social and emotional needs. Your identity merges with the abuser, as your identity outside of the relationship weakens. This creates a lack of support in recognising or taking action against the abuse. It also amplifies the effects of abuse, as you don't have a separate reality from the abuser's reality, who blames you for the abuse. This increases the feeling of distress caused by their behaviour because the person you rely on to meet your needs is the one who is abusing you, and blaming you for it.

It becomes a cycle that spirals into further isolation and dependency. Feelings of fear, shame and guilt over the loss of connection with others, and the potential for negative consequences if you reach out, prevent you from attempting to get support. This deepens the loss of connection, creating heavier dependency, amplifying the abuse, increasing feelings of shame, which prevents you reaching out... and you see how the cycle spirals and you become more and more isolated.

Loss of Connection

When you have close connections, they provide a source of independence and separate identity. Healthy connections also help to increase and maintain self-esteem. Whilst these are positive for you as an individual, they are counterproductive to the abuser's need to control. The abuser feels threatened by this and works to break these connections and create dependency.

This is primarily why the abuser aims to isolate.

More than this, friendships also provide a third-party voice. When you have close connections, you are far more likely to confide in friends if you have relationship difficulties. You are also more likely to trust their opinion. Again, this is counterproductive for the abuser. If they effectively isolate you, then they eliminate the third-party voice providing unfavourable feedback about their behaviour.

It doesn't have to be complete isolation. You might still have contact with others, but the abuser creates a level of distance or distrust. Perhaps they make it difficult for you to attend social gatherings, so you 'naturally' drop out from the inner circle. Either way, it means there is no one outside of the relationship you feel you can rely on. There is no one to flag the abuser's behaviour or support you in maintaining higher levels of self-esteem through positive interactions. There is only the abuser's voice and your own. The issue is the abuser manipulates the reality of the situation and creates doubt in your own perception. You therefore become dependent on the abuser's version of what is happening in the relationship.

Which is another imbalance of power.

Another tactic is to isolate you by manipulating other's perception of the relationship. So, you are still in contact with people, but they support the abuser's reality. They say, 'oh, don't be so hard on them', or 'well, they have already spoken to me about this, and I think you are overreacting!' Or they voice how incredible and caring the abuser is towards you. This is not only isolating through loss of connection but invalidating of your experiences. It can leave you feeling detached from others and amplify the confusion and loss of self-trust in your ability to perceive your relationship effectively. This is a common tactic in families, where the abusive family member will attempt to recruit other family members onto their side, to isolate you from getting support from their abusive behaviour within your family system. It also reinforces the abusive narrative that the problem is your reaction, not the abuser's behaviour.

Emotional, Social & Financial Dependency

Once you are isolated, you also become dependent on the abuser for emotional connection. As the abuser is possibly the only emotional bond, or at least the only unaffected one, you become dependent on them to meet your social and emotional needs. This furthers the power imbalance, as it is a far more effective tool to withdraw emotional warmth as punishment if it is your only source of connection. We need to belong, to connect with others and to feel emotional reciprocation, so it is significantly more distressing to withhold affection if we don't feel we have a positive connection in other relationships. As a result, our attempts to avoid disappointing the abuser are amplified and can feel intense, as we are also attempting to keep hold of the only relationship where we feel we still belong.

Dependency is not only developed through cutting you off socially, but also financially. Financial abuse includes controlling your access to money or creating financial instability. Where the abuser controls finances, they might limit access to bank accounts or credit cards, restrict your working hours so you cannot earn a reasonable income, or demand access to your bank accounts so they can monitor your expenditures. Where the abuser creates financial instability, they gamble recklessly, rack up debts or take out loans in your name, or spend your shared savings. Financial abuse is another element of the abusive relationship, and alongside emotional and social dependency, creates further practical barriers to leaving the relationship, due to lack of social support and financial security. These three aspects take away your options, limit your freedom of choice, and restrict your ability to function independently.

Isolation Tactics

Isolation is unlikely to be achieved through overt tactics. The abuser usually accomplishes it through subtler tactics of guilt and manipulation. They create an 'us against them' mentality, claiming nobody understands you the way they do. Or they claim friends and family don't accept them and create pressure for you to choose between your relationship with the abuser or socialising with others. They use guilt, such as claiming they have no friends in the area, to pressure you into staying with them and spending less time with your own social network. Or they suggest you are less serious about the relationship if you 'prioritise' seeing other people as frequently as you do.

This is an effective way of shifting responsibility for your isolation onto you. Later in the relationship, if you are upset about the distance in your friendships, the abuser will claim it was your choice to stop seeing your friends. They may even go one step further and tell you that you have been a poor friend because you stopped putting effort in. This is far from the truth, which is they manipulated you into becoming isolated. However, it is effective in invalidating your feelings, and fostering guilt and shame, which provides a power shift to the abuser and prevents you from reaching out and trying to reconnect.

Lack of Support

Ultimately, through isolation there is a lack of support systems in place. If the time comes a survivor wants to leave the relationship, they may literally see no options. They struggle to reach out to others, not only because of the abuse but because of the shame harboured for losing connection with them.

Even when healthy relationships end, we rely on our support systems for emotional, social, financial, or other means of support. So, consider the abusive relationship. There is a high level of control without a support system there to help you. It's not a simple act of courage and bravery to leave, although it does indeed take that. It is also a logistical question of possibility. Was it even possible to leave earlier? It is not a straightforward question of, 'why didn't I choose to leave?' but 'what prevented me from being able to leave?'.

Do not feel shame for being in an abusive relationship. You are brave and courageous for how long you stayed. You are brave and courageous if and when you leave. And you are brave and courageous, now you choose to heal.

Confusion

Confusion is the abuser's tool to create helplessness and an inability to take action. If you are in a perpetual state of doubt and confusion over the relationship, inclusive of their and your own behaviour, you become heavily reliant on the abuser's judgement and version of reality. This leads to difficulty in even identifying the behaviour as abusive, let alone holding them accountable and making choices to protect yourself from it. It means you are far more likely to stay and tolerate unacceptable behaviour. It is this confusion that keeps us mentally stuck and contributes towards why we become trapped in the relationship.

Moving Goalposts

Moving the goalposts is a tactic based on inconsistency. What satisfies the abuser one day will anger them the next. There is inconsistency in their expectations, in their attitude towards you and their mood, and in their commitment to the relationship. This keeps you on your toes, never able to settle into a rhythm or sense of security. It creates confusion over what they expect from you and how to take action to improve your situation, which is what leads to feeling helpless and shifts the power to the abuser.

Everything is a guessing game. The abuser doesn't communicate constructively but expects you to know exactly what they want and for you to meet these demands. These aren't requests but expectations fuelled by entitlement. They then berate you if you cannot read their mind. If you manage to get it right, they simply move the goalposts, so you get it wrong the next time.

It's a relationship based upon shifting rules of engagement which only the abuser is privy to and changes to suit their agenda.

Helplessness

The confusion acts as a drug to dull your cognitive abilities to think, feel and act for yourself. With so much uncertainty and abuse, the world can feel unsafe. This may cause us fear and anxiety over the smallest things. Even making seemingly irrelevant decisions, such as what to watch on TV or what to eat for dinner, can be anxiety inducing to the point we try to avoid making decisions altogether. When we make a decision, there is the potential we make the 'wrong' decision, leading to further abuse. Hence, we learn to avoid decision making and we learn helplessness.

When we recognise how high levels of fear and anxiety effect our ability to make small day-to-day decisions in an abusive relationship, to the extent we avoid them as self-protection, we can understand how fear is used to prevent us from making life-changing decisions, such as leaving the relationship. The thought of making such a significant decision can immobilise you, and that's the point of abuse.

When talking about 'allowing' abuse to happen, we often overlook that confusion created a helplessness to take action. It is not simply you ignored red flags or tolerated abuse. It's that confusion engulfs the relationship. In this atmosphere of confusion, you become immobilised to take action, as you cannot determine which way to move, who to trust, what to think, or how to feel.

When survivors reflect on the relationship, they sometimes feel they should have done more, or they should have recognised the abuse. Hindsight is a wonderful thing, but it can also create undue shame. The clarity you have post-separation is not something you were privy to at the time.

Conflicting Emotions

Another source of confusion is conflicting emotions. The abuser is far more than just their abusive behaviour to the survivor: they are a parent, sibling, romantic partner, friend, boss or other significant relationship. You have an emotional connection to who they are in their relationship role, not only who they are as a person. They are someone you feel you ought to be able to trust with your emotional vulnerability. They are someone you feel should be safe and who you want to have an emotional connection with. The emotional tie provides a platform where you fear misreading or misinterpreting their behaviour because you also fear losing that relationship. There is fear of losing them as a person, but also the fear of losing a mother, a best friend, a partner, a dream job.

The mental fog created by the confusion means you struggle to identify the abuse or whether the relationship is unhealthy. You may ask questions, such as, 'is it all in my head? Shouldn't I just be happy? What's my problem?', and therefore feel afraid to sever the emotional tie and lose them as a person as well as what they represent. How can you gauge if it is the right thing to leave, if the abuse has fostered a state of confusion and self-doubt? This again leads to feeling helpless and stuck, where you tolerate a higher level of unacceptable behaviour than you otherwise would. If you were a child, it was not even your responsibility to name the abuse and make such a difficult decision. You were in a position where you relied on adults to protect you. To not tolerate abuse towards you and intervene.

Punishment

Punishment is a key part of the abusive relationship in stoking fear or shame within you and limiting your use of free will. The abusive relationship thrives on fear and shame. Fear to speak up, fear to tolerate it, fear to leave, fear to stay, fear for safety, fear of loss, fear of harm, fear of consequences, fear of unworthiness, fear of blame and the shame associated with all of this. The fear that you're going crazy. So much fear is connected to the threat of being punished. So, you try to be exactly who the abuser wants, rather than be an individual in your own right and risk punishment.

Moulding Behaviour

The fear of punishment is a powerful way to regulate and mould your behaviour. If you are afraid to screw a jam jar lid too tight, then taking action to leave seems impossible for fear of the consequences. And with good reason. Abusers can become volatile at the point of separation and threaten or imply they will destroy you if you break away from their control. They threaten to target your reputation, or your mental, physical, social, or financial security. Nothing is off limits, and this threat is a powerful tool to make you stay in the relationship.

As well as the threat of increased abuse, such as incessant criticism, explosive rage, silent treatment or the threat of physical harm, abusers threaten other consequences. These include threatening to take your children away, to make you homeless, to turn family members against you or harass people you care about, making false accusations to the police or even threatening suicide. Abusers threaten consequences they feel you are most afraid of. These are all forms of punishment. The abuser sends the message you will do as they say, otherwise there will be dire consequences for you. It also sends the message that your fate is in your hands; you will be to blame because your actions, such as your decision to leave, led to the consequence. It prevents you from being able to make rational decisions to protect yourself because it creates a reality where you feel the best form of protection is to ensure you do not upset the abuser.

This is something we can highlight for ourselves and others. When asking why you didn't leave an abusive relationship, staying may have felt like the least risky option.

Pre-occupation with Avoiding Harm

With the fear of punishment develops a pre-occupation with avoiding harm. The fear of consequences and subsequent urge to avoid harm leads to you becoming preoccupied with your every move. Analysing it, trying to think five steps ahead, going over and over whether it's your fault, beating yourself up about the smallest of things. So much of the abuse and the behaviour becomes internalised. This not only keeps self-esteem low, but it also brings shame into the relationship. We fear the harmful consequences and also feel ashamed because we internalise the blame for them.

Whilst you are preoccupied with whether your own behaviour is acceptable, you do not have the energy to invest in recognising their behaviour as abuse. Think of it like a magician's misdirection. It is the abuser's trick to distract you from being able to focus on, call out and hold them accountable for their abuse by (mis)directing your attention towards your own behaviour. You become preoccupied with yourself and your every move to avoid further harm, which simultaneously keeps the heat off the abuser.

Control

Control is the fourth cornerstone and central to the abusive relationship. Through the other cornerstones of isolation, confusion and punishment, an environment is established where the abuser can exert control. Isolation creates dependency and a lack of support, confusion creates an inability to take action, and punishment establishes a fear of consequences. Within this environment, patterns of abusive behaviour, pressure and a power imbalance are all used as tools to control.

Abuse centres around the abuser's need for control and using harmful or dysfunctional ways to achieve it.

Power & Control

Control sedates the abuser's feeling of powerlessness or satisfies their feeling of entitlement to power. Every time something highlights the feeling of powerlessness, it amplifies their need to have control. The abuser responds with severe behaviour, subjecting you to explosive rages or extreme displays of emotions, such as anger, tears, or silence. These are attempts to regain control over the situation by overpowering you and eliciting a submissive response from you.

In her book Power and Control, Sandra Horley discusses how there are multiple ways in which the abuser will use control to shift the power balance in the relationship. Maybe they always have to be in charge. Or, they always must have the last word, control the finances, isolate you, put you down, blame you, show extreme jealousy, don't allow a sense of separateness, use fear or manipulation or make you feel crazy.

These behaviours mean the power in the relationship is always advantaged to the abuser.

It is important to recognise how survivors empower themselves whilst in a disempowering environment. We often place expectations from healthier relationships on survivors and feel they should have made 'better' choices to protect themselves. In fact, this is not possible because of the environment they are in. As a survivor, you adapt, and you make choices to protect yourself even in this hostile environment. You learn when to keep your head down, you try to steal happy moments for yourself and periods of respite when the abuser is away from you. You try to counter the abuse by being a nurturing parent or trying to develop a sense of identity through a hobby. It is not the same as leaving, but in the relationship's context, it is important to recognise that you were always making choices to survive, to minimise harm and find subtle ways to empower yourself.

Coercive Control

Women's Aid, a leading UK charity for women who have experienced domestic abuse, describes coercive control as 'a pattern of assault, threats, humiliation and intimidation' to create fear and dependency. Common behaviours include isolation, threats, monitoring, sexual coercion, physical violence, financial abuse and depriving you of access to support, such as attending your medical appointments.

This type of control is also present through your day-to-day interactions. It is important to recognise it is not only big displays of overtly harmful behaviour that are abusive. Your every move might be under scrutiny and control, including what you wear, what you eat, or how you brush your teeth. This is monitoring through micromanagement.

The abuser micromanages any and every aspect of your life.

Micromanaging how you behave socially

The abuser monitors how you talk to your friends, what you say to others, or even your facial expressions. They accuse you of speaking or acting condescendingly towards them or making an embarrassment of yourself. They claim they cannot trust you to behave appropriately around others or that you become disrespectful and should 'know your place' or 'treat them better'. Or, they control what you wear, where you go, when you go out and who you go out with.

Micromanaging how you behave at home

This can include the smallest of details, such as how you apply toothpaste to your toothbrush or place post on the table. Expecting you to cook a new recipe every meal, and to have it ready the exact time they arrive home, with no indication when that will be. Even managing how you speak, the language you use, the way you laugh, how you sit, what you watch, how you clean, how much time you spend in the shower, how you apply your makeup or how you shave. The atmosphere is one of walking on eggshells, where the abuser micromanages any part of who you are and what you are doing.

This creates a negative cycle further into the power imbalance: because of the power imbalance that is already established you try to think ten steps ahead, monitoring your own behaviour and trying to please the abuser, with the aim of avoiding further criticism and negative consequences. This spirals you further into their control and micromanagement because you can no longer think and act freely.

Micromanaging finances

Controlling finances is an effective way of maintaining control, as it prevents you from having financial independence and stability. Leaving becomes much harder if you cannot support yourself financially or face homelessness. The abuser may micromanage finances by controlling access to money or hiding your debit card. They expect you to give them updates of your finances and to account for any excess or shortage of money. They might not even allow you to have a separate account. Or, they themselves secretly save money whilst putting minimal into the joint household budget so they are in a financial position of power. Alternatively, they gamble or spend recklessly to prevent you from saving.

So, coming back to the original question of 'Why didn't I leave?' Practical barriers, fear of consequences, lack of social support, inability to trust your perception, financial dependence, high levels of control, loss of identity, chronic self-doubt, and the emotional connection, are just some of the many reasons. When we feel trapped in an unsafe environment, we spend our energy trying to survive and minimise the harm of the current situation. And that is energy well spent. It is certainly nothing to be ashamed of.

5 things to consider when leaving an abusive relationship:

- o Talking to the abuser about abuse equips them with information to use against you and accuse you of. Do not assume they don't know what they're doing.
- o Telling the abuser how they've hurt you equips them with information to cause you greater pain.
- o The abuser might go to excessive lengths to make it difficult for you to break free. Make an exit plan. Share as little information as possible with them.
- o Outside sources, such as family courts, social workers and mediators, may lose understanding of the severity of abuse because they have to maintain a position of neutrality. They will believe the abuser to varying degrees, which is a further source of pain and invalidation. At a time when you feel emotionally vulnerable, you need to present yourself as factually and rationally as possible.
- o Friendships are difficult to maintain and rebuild. You lose friendships that were formed during the abusive relationship and those that were lost during the relationship have to be restored.

...and most importantly, through all the challenges and all the despair, it is worth it.

Chapter two:

Acknowledgement

With a deeper understanding of abusive relationships, you can reflect on your own experiences and acknowledge whether abuse was present. This provides a baseline of clarity. Some survivors find this initial acknowledgement distressing, as they could not identify the behaviour as abusive whilst they were experiencing it. It's like the floodgates opening when you realise the abuse, and the intensity of emotions can feel overwhelming. For others, it's a more gradual acknowledgement; a slow confirmation of what you already knew deep down.

You need to remember; you did your best with the knowledge, awareness, and resources you had to handle the situation. Be as compassionate with your emotions and vulnerability as you can.

One caution is seeking to identify every type of abusive behaviour you learn of, in your own relationship, to validate your pain and your experiences. This is a slippery slope and I'll tell you why. It becomes a sticking point to believing your own experiences.

They didn't isolate me.

They never lost their temper.

They didn't cheat on me.

It can't be abuse because these things don't fit the description.

No relationship is going to consist of all abusive behaviours. You will gain an awareness of certain types of abuse, behaviours and patterns that were not present in your relationship. Does it make your relationship less abusive? No. It makes it individual. No two relationships are the same. Abuse is not comparable. It is not about who had it worse. Your pain is valid.

If you get into the habit of trying to 'tick box' every abusive behaviour to accept you have experienced abuse, you are setting yourself up for further emotional pain. It turns into a negative cycle of trying to self-soothe through ticking off the abuse checklist. When you can't check something off, it provokes distress, which leads to you trying to self-soothe by reading more to tick off abusive behaviours again... which inevitably leads to further distress.

It is difficult in the early stages because of self-doubt and lack of self-trust. The key to acknowledgment is when something resonates you say, 'yes, I acknowledge I have experienced this'. When something doesn't resonate you say, 'that wasn't a part of my relationship', without it shaking your truth that there were other abusive behaviours present.

When you acknowledge there was abuse in your relationship, follow-up questions emerge. These include the abuser's understanding of their own actions, their motivation and whether they even know they're abusive. Also, if they are abusive without even knowing, the question many fear is, 'does that mean I could be the abusive one without even realising it?'

Question: Do They do it on Purpose?

This is the million-dollar question. Are they abusive on purpose? It's an interesting question because in terms of moral compass it makes a vast difference. If they are abusive on purpose (evil even) then they are morally bankrupt, and you can cut ties. Right? But if they are unknowingly abusive… do they require empathy? Understanding? Are you obliged to tolerate abuse because they don't know any better? It becomes a far more complex question of how to perceive them and their behaviour. To this I say, although it may affect the level of empathy you feel towards them, it does not make a difference to whether it is a safe relationship for you.

Evil Intention?

To answer the question, 'do they do it on purpose': yes… and not entirely.

There are different reasons people are abusive. Psychopaths are aware of moral choices, but do not feel anguish at causing harm to others. Therefore, they make a logical decision about how to act based on what benefits them most, including choosing to harm you. They know it's morally wrong; they know it will cause you harm, but if it benefits them, they still feel it's the best choice and will go for it.

However, not all abusers are psychopaths.

There are underlying factors that need to be considered. It may be (harmful) self-protection or a sense of entitlement, which has led to the abuser adopting abusive behaviour and dominance over another person. Or an abusive mentality developed through certain deep-rooted beliefs. Often, it is a combination of factors with varying levels or awareness and intention. So yes, they do it on purpose, but their level of conscious awareness varies.

Here, I put to you, they will see the effects of their behaviour. They will see the impact on your mental health, the distress it causes, and your attempts to communicate to them about how you are feeling. They have the chance to know better and a responsibility over their behaviour. They can choose to control it. So, whether they consciously choose to inflict harm or not, at some point they are aware and therefore choosing to continue to engage in abusive behaviour. Abuse is the choice of the abuser, regardless of what extent they do it on purpose.

Gender Stereotypes

There is evidence abuse is the product of unhealthy core beliefs and values, including unhealthy attitudes and stereotypes towards gender. One study found men who grew up with family or friends who had negative gender role beliefs were more likely to be abusive toward women. These negative beliefs towards gender tie into the abuser's attitudes of:

a) how they have the right to be treated

b) how they are entitled to behave

c) the behaviour they expect from others

For example, a man with rigid gender stereotyping believes he has a basic right to be treated with greater respect than women, encouraged by the beliefs of his father, or other male role model, and his experiences of male privilege. He feels, not only should women show him the respect he deserves, but he is also entitled to treat women disrespectfully, because of their lower status based on their gender. This belief leads him to expect submissive behaviour in his relationships, whilst he is entitled to discipline and behave abusively towards the women he dates.

It is not only heterosexual women who are abused because of negative gender beliefs. A man could be shamed for not 'fulfilling' the gender stereotype, being labelled too sensitive and derided for not providing adequately. The female abuser takes a position of self-righteousness, believing she is fulfilling her gender expectations whilst the man falls short. The shaming affects his self-worth, which leads to the power imbalance and the abuser dominating the relationship.

In LGBTQIA+ relationships, although less commonly than in heterosexual relationships, couples might take on traditional masculine and feminine roles, therefore also experiencing abuse driven by the beliefs of rigid gender stereotyping. Or children are abused because of the abusive parent's rigid expectations based on their child's gender. More than this, a child might lack parental acceptance and face higher criticism, based on their gender and the abusive parent's belief of one gender being superior.

The rigid views on gender roles mean the abuser feels self-righteous. They feel superior based on their gender, or morally superior as they believe they are fulfilling their gender role, whilst believing you aren't fulfilling yours. They hold rigid views on how they are entitled to be treated and how they are entitled to behave, based on your and their gender. In their mind, this justifies their criticism and abusive behaviour towards you. Although it doesn't answer whether they abuse on purpose, it provides rigid gender stereotyping as an underlying cause of abuse.

Are Abusers Angry?

Would you believe me if I was to tell you abuse isn't anger driven?

Abusers don't lose their temper. It isn't in the heat of the moment. A display of anger is a staged mechanism to create a submissive response in you. They use fear and the risk of punishment or harm to gain control. One study into abusive men found they were driven by a social need to control, not anger. This theory is supported by the Freedom Programme, a domestic abuse programme developed by Pat Craven. The programme evolved from her work with male perpetrators of domestic violence, and she found abusers were not angry, but in control of their emotions and thinking clearly.

This makes an interesting argument against the use of anger management programmes for abusers. Anger management suggests they have a problem with controlling their anger when the actual issue they have a problem with is their need to control. Anger management isn't addressing the issue and can imply we provoke their anger. This reinforces the victim blaming mentality of the abuser and allows them to remain in denial about the root cause of their harmful behaviour to avoid accountability.

Furthermore, struggling with poor mental health is not a cause of abusive behaviour. There are many people in the world with mental health conditions who are not abusive. Just how they blame you for their anger, some abusers use the excuse of poor mental health to avoid accountability for their actions. We feel obliged to stand by someone who is struggling, blaming their mental health condition for their actions rather than holding them responsible. They therefore avoid working on core issues that drive abusive behaviour, such as the need for control, entitlement, and deep-rooted beliefs.

Sabotaging Behaviour

Some abusers will engage in sabotaging behaviours. These behaviours are deceptive and leave you questioning whether you are being paranoid or whether they are doing it on purpose, which adds to your confusion, self-doubt, anxiety and instability, leading to further mental deterioration.

Sabotaging to avoid responsibilities

The abuser sabotages their own efforts to meet their responsibilities in the relationship. This can include emotional, practical or financial responsibilities to avoid having any. They cook an inedible meal or take you on a date skydiving when they know you're afraid of heights. When you react unfavourably, they use this to justify why you should take on all responsibilities and why they should have none. According to you (ahem) 'nothing is ever good enough'.

Expecting a fair distribution of responsibilities in your relationships is healthy. However, if you ask the abuser to take on an equal number of responsibilities, you are also creating a more equal distribution of power. The aim of the abuser is to prevent you from asking again by sabotaging their own efforts and blaming you for their lack of effort. It's manipulation to accommodate their entitled behaviour and need for power and control.

Sabotaging to create instability

The abuser sabotages your efforts to function in your day-to-day life. Some abusers enjoy playing games to mess with your head. They will move your belongings around the house and watch you become frantic as you search for them or hide their own belongings and watch you panic when they blame you for it. They gain satisfaction from the power trip they get from throwing you off kilter. You may clock a smirk on their face when you feel in utter distress. As a result, not only is there a lack of stability in the relationship, but also in the environment. This further takes away your feeling of safety.

Sabotaging to manipulate perception

Sabotaging behaviour also extends beyond the relationship as abusers sabotage your connection with others. This is not only achieved though isolation but also by manipulating public perception. The abuser has a different public persona than behind closed doors and may even suggest to others you are unstable, or they are 'worried' about your mental state. As people aren't aware of the abusive dynamic, they misread your emotions in public as evidence that supports the abuser's narrative. Therefore, they believe the abuser is stable and supportive whilst you are struggling to cope, rather than realising that any appearance of instability is because of the abuse you endure behind closed doors.

Different Goals

It is important to recognise the conflicting goals in an abusive relationship. A healthy goal is to want harmony in the relationship. The goal of the abuser is to have control through harmful behaviours. What you say or do does not change their need to control. And if you do everything they ask for willingly, it doesn't satisfy their need to control. Therefore, nothing seems enough, and the goalposts always move. Whilst your goal is to repair, their goal is to maintain the power imbalance.

It was nothing you said or did that caused the abuse. Their behaviour originates in them and their drive for control.

Understanding the different goals in the abusive relationship helps you to identify that you are not to blame for the abusive behaviour. More than this, shifting focus onto the impact of their behaviour rather than whether they do it on purpose can support you in identifying that it was abuse. Whilst you naturally want to understand why it happened, when you focus on the abuser, you can form a great hypothesis but never get a definitive answer. This is disempowering. You can, however, be certain of the impact it had on you, and therefore empower yourself through shifting your focus to reflect on:

- Did I feel safe?
- Was my self-esteem affected?
- Did my mental health decline?
- Did I become isolated?
- Did I start to question my character?
- Did I feel confused all the time?
- Was I scared of their temper?
- Did I hide their behaviour from others or try to reason it to myself?

Focusing on the impact brings clarity as to whether the behaviour was harmful. This helps you to acknowledge what you've experienced and whether the relationship was safe. It brings more peace of mind than chasing the answer to the abuser's intentions, which often leads to more questions and uncertainty.

5 reflective questions to shift focus onto growth:

- o Is this a safe relationship for me?
- o Are they able to recognise their behaviour is harmful?
- o Do they try to adopt healthier behaviours (not just empty words or empty actions)?
- o What steps can I take to protect myself?
- o What steps can I take to protect my environment?

Question: Am I the Abusive One?

Abusers may have fleeting moments of considering whether they are abusive, but they push it out, squash it down, rationalise, or deny quicker than the thought can materialise. When survivors go through the process of recovery, they are thrown into a period of major transition, and part of that process is extensive self-reflection. To make sense of abusive narratives and gain stability again, we self-reflect. We search to understand the confusion of what we thought we understood and what we are coming to understand. We also self-reflect to self-protect; to assess what has happened and how we can heal to avoid it in the future. We self-reflect and embark on this journey because we want to resolve the pain of being abused. Abusers do not embark on this journey because the relationship was not traumatic for them.

A fixation on, 'am I the abusive one?', is a continuation of the abusive message. It is what the abuser would like you to believe. It hinders you from being able to do the self-reflective work to heal and grow and prevents you from acknowledging the extent of their abusive behaviour. When you lack clarity about who was abusive in the relationship, you cannot get past the fear that you are the abuser.

Projecting Abuse

Throughout the relationship, the abuser will project their abusive behaviours onto you. They may constantly criticise you and accuse you of being overly critical or they are excessively jealous and accuse you of being jealous about their relationships. They fly into unpredictable rages and accuse you of being unable to control your emotions. This means when you self-reflect, you remember being told you were critical, jealous, or exploding with rage, which all fit the profile of an abuser. When in fact, it was the abuser projecting their own behaviour onto you, rather than a genuine assessment of how you were behaving.

Further to this, the abuser places responsibility for their behaviour and the toxic environment on you. They say it is your reactions that cause tension, your perception is wrong or your behaviour that led to the abusive incident. This leads to you internalising the blame for the abuse and the environment. In an abusive relationship, the abuser does not allow you to have a separate self, so you may have experienced a loss of identity through the tactics of isolation, confusion, and control. If you don't have a strong sense of who you are anymore, you are vulnerable to internalising the projection and blame, and believe you could be an abuser without knowing it.

No Flaws Allowed

In an abusive relationship, any perceived flaws come under intense scrutiny. Over time, you learn to view your own behaviour through the same lens as the abuser and scrutinise the smallest of shortcomings. You beat yourself mercilessly for simple errors and this can lead to over-inflating and labelling your own behaviour as abusive, when it is simply because you are human.

Be gentle with yourself.

In the early stages, many survivors go through a period of panic when they are still building self-trust and working through the confusion. They read about abusive behaviour and identify it in themselves. They read an abuser will harbour money and control finances to create a power imbalance and think, 'I started saving money behind my abuser's back to escape, does that make me abusive?'

The answer is no.

The power imbalance in abusive relationships means not all actions are equal. When you yell at the abuser, it does not have the same effect as when the abuser yells at you. You might yell as you are trying to protect yourself and likely feeling significant distress. The abuser yells as part of the abuse. They are trying to overpower you and often feel calm, even though they appear full of rage.

The response is different too. You experience high levels of anxiety, fear, helplessness, and distress. Although the abuser feels a threat to their authority being challenged or threat to their ego, they will not feel distress in the same way because they hold significant power in the relationship. They might even enjoy seeing you lose your temper, as this signifies the power they have over you through causing you to 'lose control' of your emotions.

It's not always possible to behave the way you want in a toxic environment. It is important for you to self-reflect on your behaviour in the context of being abused and extend kindness and understanding to yourself. You may have picked up unhealthy behaviours to survive. *That's ok*. You are capable of healing. In the early stages, however, gaining clarity of your experiences rather than deep diving into self-reflection, will help you to feel grounded rather than create further distress, confusion, and shame. It will help you to process your pain rather than bypass it and feel over-responsible for the relationship tensions.

Know this: just because you made mistakes, doesn't mean you deserved abuse. Just because you could have handled a situation better, doesn't mean you weren't worthy of love. *You are not the cause of their abuse.* They abuse because they choose to. And if you secretly save to escape, or shut down communication, need to know every detail of a plan, or read into every word people say to feel safe, this doesn't make you abusive or controlling. Being flawed, which we all are, doesn't make you abusive. When you can recognise this, it supports you in acknowledging the abuse in your relationship, without internalising the blame for its presence.

5 affirmations to be gentle with yourself:

o   It was not my fault.
o   I deserved better.
o   I am here for you (for myself).
o   I was and I am enough.
o   I am safe now.

Chapter three:

Acceptance

Acknowledgement of abuse leads the way to acceptance: of the experience, how you feel, and the impact of the relationship. Many survivors struggle with being able to accept how devastated, how broken, or how traumatised they feel. They berate and shame themselves for having a powerful reaction and not being able to 'just get over it'. They apply the logic of what they would expect of themselves when recovering from a healthy relationship.

When you acknowledge the abuse in your experiences, you can accept the depth of your response. It is proportionate; it is valid. And you are certainly not broken.

Acceptance is not accepting it was ok. It is becoming aware of, acknowledging, and accepting your truth. Acceptance allows you to rebuild how you understand your experiences, your relationships, your emotions and your world to gain a sense of stability once again. It is with acceptance you can plant your seeds of growth to heal from the effects of abuse.

Question: Am I Overreacting?

After abuse, it is common to wonder whether you are oversensitive or whether your response to abuse has been an overreaction. The abuser may have told you this, to shift blame and avoid accountability, or perhaps people you know who apply their own point of view to the relationship.

People say, 'maybe they didn't mean any harm', or, 'I'm sure there's a reasonable explanation'. They may say it intending to comfort you, but it actually has the opposite effect. Rather than calming, it can cause further distress as it invalidates your experiences. It reinforces the fear you have indeed overreacted to a 'normal' situation, which would also reinforce the message it is your reaction that causes the conflict, not the abusive behaviour. This is partly why we search to know our reaction is proportionate and justified.

When a healthy relationship ends, there is a period of transition. This is a significant and challenging time, but our understanding of the relationship and ourselves remains constant. When an abusive relationship ends, it is not only the transition that comes with relationship endings to cope with, but your understanding of the relationship and yourself does not remain constant. It becomes unstable. This makes the impact of the transition acutely more significant and therefore, you cannot compare your reaction, response, or sensitivity towards it to how you would cope with the end of a healthy relationship.

Long-Term Effects

In an abusive relationship, you have been living for an extended period in survival mode.

You cannot simply switch survival mode on and off. It has complex implications for the way you process information, respond and interact and effects your emotional, psychological and physiological responses. Long-term effects of emotional abuse include depression, anxiety and chronic pain, as well as developing low self-esteem and feelings of guilt and shame. It is also connected to issues such as substance abuse, heart disease, eating disorders, or other mental health conditions. Whilst not all survivors of abuse develop complex post-traumatic stress disorder (CPTSD), many report symptoms of it, including hypervigilance, dissociation, flashbacks, insomnia, nightmares and high anxiety, as well as difficulty regulating emotions.

There is more to heal from an abusive relationship than just losing it. You are also healing from the effects of abuse and the relationship itself.

Healthy relationships do not erode your self-esteem and your mental wellbeing. You shouldn't experience a high level of doubt and confusion over the behaviour that took place throughout the relationship. To experience such a high level of doubt and confusion *indicates abuse in itself*. Also, living in a state of nervousness because of the other person's erratic or unpredictable moods. Never feeling like you are good enough or you can do anything right. What was acceptable one week not being acceptable the next. The goalposts always changing, and feeling unable to fall into a rhythm of knowing what they expect from you. Feeling unhappy, scared or confused, but not being able to explain why. Feeling hollow or that you don't recognise yourself anymore. Or feeling detached from the world. These are all indications of being subjected to abusive behaviour.

Just as if our diet consisted of toxic foods, it would have a long-term impact on our health, being in a sustained abusive environment has long-term effects on our wellbeing. Your diet isn't only what you eat, it is also what you internalise from your environment, and whether this is healthy or unhealthy will impact accordingly on your wellbeing. Do not burden yourself with the expectation you should have handled it differently or had a different reaction. Your reaction is valid. It's OK to be affected by abuse.

It's OK to not be Ok.

Allow yourself that, so you can show yourself kindness for the impact it has had, get the support you need and focus on healing.

Loss

There is a significant amount of loss in an abusive relationship. This can include the loss of friendships, family support, your home, or anything else connected to your life. There is also the loss of self. There is a loss of self-esteem, hopes and happiness, and self-identity or feeling like you deserve better. When your identity has been steadily eroded throughout the relationship, you may only feel a strong sense of identity in connection to the abuser. When you lose their love, attention or approval, this can feel like the ultimate loss because it feels like it's all you had left.

If the relationship with the abuser ends, you may come to a point where you feel shame or frustration that you aren't 'over it'. However, maybe it's not that you can't move on from the relationship, it's that you're still affected by the abuse. It's not that you can't let go of them, it's that you're grieving the loss of what they represented for you. It's not that you are lost, it's that you are learning who you are without them. And you are healing.

To sum up, it is not an overreaction to be affected by the abuse and loss. There is much to heal from and there is no time scale. There is no right or wrong way to respond or be affected. We are each unique, so in that way our experiences and healing also have a uniqueness. Be brave and honour what feels right for you, accepting guidance and support along the way, but also rejecting the ideas that don't fit with your own healing.

5 reflections for validating your responses:

- o My emotions are valid.
- o It is OK when I have down days, even after feeling good. This is not a setback. It is a part of the process.
- o I will not pressure myself by holding my healing to a time frame.
- o I understand my responses are because of my experiences and will show self-compassion.
- o I will allow myself to rest because I know my growth is long term.

SURVIVOR'S GUIDE

THE THREE A'S TAKEAWAYS:

· Emotional abuse targets your feelings. Psychological abuse targets your thoughts. Both can result from the same abusive behaviour and significantly impact wellbeing.

· The abusive relationship consists of micro and macro patterns of abuse, which create a tapestry of pressure to mould your behaviour to please the abuser.

· Single incidents lose the significance of the impact of sustained abuse. It is important to consider behaviour in the relationship's context to recognise the extent of abuse.

· The abuser creates a power imbalance through the cornerstones of abuse: isolation, confusion, punishment (fear) and control.

· Unique aspects drive abusive behaviour, including the need to control, unhealthy beliefs and values, and negative gender stereotyping.

· Shifting focus onto the impact of abuse rather than the abuser's intentions empowers you to acknowledge abuse in your relationship.

· The power imbalance means not all actions are equal between yourself and the abuser. Losing your temper or showing other behaviours which seem similar, does not make you abusive.

· An abusive relationship has a significant impact because you also need to process an unclear understanding of yourself and your experiences. There are the effects of abuse on your wellbeing and overarching losses in your life, in the relationship, and within yourself.

· Acceptance of your experiences helps you regain a sense of stability in your emotions, your perception, and your world and facilitates the path towards growth and healing.

· There is no one size fits all for healing. Your responses are valid, your emotions are valid, and your healing is unique.

The Three A's Journal Prompt

I have gained awareness of...

I acknowledge my experience of...

I will accept my feeling of...

Part Two

Untangling Self

Do you give yourself a hard time over how you felt, behaved, or what you brought into the relationship? Do you criticise yourself for your current thoughts and feelings because you still feel attached or unable to trust yourself? It can feel like we yo-yo between moments of profound clarity and the blurry haze of confusion. We feel uncertainty about ourselves, as much as whether it was even abuse.

In a relationship that sustained itself on amplifying your confusion, give yourself the grace of self-compassion for not suddenly being able to stand with confidence in the truth of your experiences.

To understand how and why abuse affects us the way it does, I am going to adapt the Cycle of Abuse. This is a great resource for understanding the abusive dynamic, as it defines abusive behaviour in four phases and how we are affected in the cycle of abuse. Through this recognition we can ease shame and confusion over how we behave in abusive relationships and how they continue to affect us.

Another great resource is the Power and Control Wheel, which highlights how a drive for power and control is central and always present in abusive relationships. Even caring or romantic behaviour in an abuse dynamic has an underlying drive for power and control. It shows how abuse permeates key aspects of life, through economic abuse, isolation, intimidation, manipulation, coercion and emotional abuse.

The Cycle of Abuse names the four phases as: tension building, incident, reconciliation, and calm. However, with power and control central to the abusive dynamic, I will refer to each category to highlight its significance:

- Building Tension
- Acute Pressure
- Manipulation
- Trauma Bonding

Not all survivors will experience the cycle of abuse in its four phases. Some do not experience a 'honeymoon' period. Instead, the abuser's behaviour jumps straight from abusive incident back to tension building behaviours that have you walking on eggshells. Others do not experience a climatic abusive incident. Instead, they experience ever building tensions that simmer down and rise again. Even if you recognise a cycle, many behaviours, such as tension building patterns or manipulation, are present throughout the cycle and are not only present in one given phase.

Although I have sectioned the behaviours into four, we will not consider them as four separate phases, but as four separate categories of abusive behaviour. This is because how you have experienced these categories of behaviour will be unique to you. It may have been in a cycle, it may have overlapped, or it may be that one category of behaviour far outweighs another. However, in an abusive relationship, a drive for power and control is always present. This offers an understanding why you might have felt unhappy, depressed, numb or another way you didn't understand, even though you felt they weren't being abusive at the time.

When you understand the abusive dynamic, you also gain clarity on the responses elicited by abusive behaviour, which can often feel confusing when you lack understanding of the dynamic and the impact it has. This enables you to gain a deeper understanding of yourself and to distinguish between abusive behaviour and trauma responses. Some responses resemble the behaviour of the abuser, and this can lead to shame. There is a difficulty in separating yourself, leaving you feeling you are 'just as bad' as the abuser.

Although abuse doesn't affect all survivors identically, there are responses to abuse we can discuss, that as a survivor you may recognise. This will help you untangle your responses from their abusive behaviour and to gain clarity on your feelings and how abuse has affected you. You can learn about the impact on your wellbeing and the reactions you have had, and this will help you show greater compassion to yourself for how you responded, rather than expecting yourself to have reacted differently.

It is with self-compassion you can move away from shame and towards accepting how you coped with abuse.

It is from a place of accepting ourselves that we grow.

I'm going to thank the unhealthy parts of self that helped me survive and honour them through healing.

Chapter four:

Building Tension

Emotional and psychological abusers create an environment where there is a constant feeling of internal unease. What was acceptable last week may not be acceptable tomorrow. Behaviours that originally helped you avoid criticism become the cause of it. You try to go unnoticed because they say you are too loud. They then say you're dull. They say you made a fool of yourself after one glass of wine, so you stop drinking. Now you're uptight and no fun. You try to keep the house clean; you don't do it well enough. You try to cuddle, you're too needy. When you keep your distance; you must be hiding something. You make an effort with your appearance; you must be cheating on them. When you wear slouchy clothes, they say you've let yourself go. Every single detail of who you are and what you do comes under scrutiny.

This builds tension, not only within the relationship, but within you.

These behaviours act as a constant undercurrent in the relationship, to create a power imbalance, a fear of upsetting the abuser and undermining your self-worth. You may notice subtle shifts in their behaviour, which signal the tension is escalating, so you begin 'walking on eggshells' to avoid further escalation or a more overt incident of abuse.

The key here is to understand you are not the cause of their behaviour. Building tensions tips the balance of power because your behaviour, your focus and your energy shifts towards trying to act in a way that appeases the abuser. This is the goal of the abuser. They are like the Ruler of the Castle, sitting back on their throne whilst you run around trying to avoid their entitled disdain. Or an Emotionally Stunted Child, teetering on the verge of volatile outbursts and tantrums, whilst you tiptoe around trying not to upset them.

Tension Building Behaviours

Abusers use tension building behaviours for power and control, because where there is conflict, there is the opportunity to create a power imbalance. We build a harmonious relationship on degrees of mutuality: mutual understanding, mutual respect, mutual compromise, and along with this would be a relative mutual distribution of power. All relationships go through power struggles, where two people need to work with one another, finding understanding and compromise. However, in the abusive relationship, the abuser uses power to dominate and disrespectful tactics to lower your self-esteem.

The abuser builds tension by focusing negatively on you. It's a negative outlook on who you are, how you behave, what you do, or any other factor about you. They may not say it outright, but their behaviour implies it is because of you there are tensions in the relationship. The focus is on all your perceived shortcomings or wrongdoings, rather than the abusive behaviour. This can leave you feeling, if only you could 'stop messing up' or 'making them mad', things would be OK, placing the responsibility for their behaviour on your shoulders.

Some abusers are skilled at winding up the level of tension, so you're full of nervous energy... only for nothing to happen. It has the effect of you feeling irrational, or 'it's all in your head', and seems to support the narrative that you're 'crazy'. This leads you to question your perception of the reality of the situation.

The truth is: the abuse was the setup.

I was once told by a Domestic Violence Advocate an abuser will do the least work as possible to achieve their desired outcome. You may find, once the abuser establishes a fear of abuse escalating, the abuse shifts towards the hint that an escalated incident will occur. They achieve this through subtle changes in their behaviour which build tension, such as becoming more critical, more dismissive, or changes to their body language. In response, you also alter your behaviour to prepare for the escalated incident. You become hyper aware, you tread on eggshells not to upset them, and you mind how you communicate... This has already achieved the desired outcome. They have created a situation where they have power and control without even needing to put the effort into an escalated incident of abuse.

You are not to blame for the rising tensions. Your perception isn't off. You are not irrational, and you haven't misread the situation. The abuser does not intend to resolve conflict, but to justify their behaviour and have the upper hand.

Critical Behaviours

- Criticism
- Nit-picking
- Fault finding
- Sarcasm
- Accusations
- High demands
- Jealousy
- Exaggerating your flaws

Critical behaviours hold you to unrealistic expectations and leave you feeling no matter what you do, you can do nothing right. These behaviours are highly critical and accusatory, with the underlying notion that your intention or behaviour is always negative and to blame. It can leave you feeling you had better not breathe in too deeply for fear of drawing attention to how you breathe and being criticised for it.

The barrage of critical behaviours disempowers you in the relationship because it creates a feeling of helplessness. You feel under attack for everything you do, *no matter what you do*, and therefore helpless to prevent it. Helplessness may present as trying to be invisible to avoid further disdain, or perhaps even 'giving up' on being treated better. Almost accepting the abusive behaviour as inevitable. Although it feels helpless, these are two forms of trying to protect yourself from further criticism and preserve energy. You are protecting yourself by gaining minimal attention.

There is no need to feel shame or believe you didn't stand up for yourself when you were trying to self-protect.

There is also a sense of helplessness because of the critical behaviour shifting blame onto you for the tension. You gain the feeling you have the power to stop the criticism if you stop behaving in ways that provoke it. But no matter what you do and how hard you try, you can't figure out how to 'get it right'.

Demeaning Behaviours

- Insults
- Jokes at your expense
- Derogatory names
- Belittling pet names
- Belittling your accomplishments
- Dismissive behaviour
- Undermining you
- Humiliation

Demeaning behaviours target your self-worth and invalidate you. These behaviours attack your self-esteem from several angles: your opinions, your achievements, your beliefs and values, your appearance, your capabilities, your feelings, and so on. Demeaning behaviour works to invalidate your sense of self, across all aspects of how you identify with yourself, so your sense of self-worth is gradually lowered.

Abusers also have subtle ways of demeaning you in front of others, such as a certain look or tone that is only apparent to you. This has the added component of being abused in public and feeling as though people either don't support you or that you are being irrational. It again lowers self-esteem, increases the feeling of being isolated and invalidates your feelings. It feeds into the confusion and mistrust in your own perception, creating further dependence on the abuser's reality, as doubt in your own perception of your experiences grows.

Unpredictable Behaviours

- Starting arguments for the sake of it
- Reacting negatively to positive news (or vice versa)
- Unpredictable or erratic moods
- Communicating in a confusing or contradictory way
- Lack of respect for personal boundaries
- Using information gained about you to be confrontational

Unpredictable behaviours create a lack of consistency in the environment, so you cannot gain a sense of stability or security in the relationship. This means you can never let your guard down, relax and feel at ease to be yourself. There is the air of possibility that the atmosphere could unexpectedly flip, or their mood could suddenly change. There is the expectation for you to mind read or pre-empt their unpredictable behaviour. The abuser implies the issue is obvious, when in fact it is highly unpredictable, inconsistent, or even manufactured by them, and there is no reliable way for you to foresee the incident.

It seems to just come out of nowhere.

Untangling Self (Tensions)

One of the most obvious behaviours survivors recognise in themselves, that feels the same as the abuser building tension, is having erratic or dysregulated emotions. This is where you struggle to manage your emotional responses.

When you are experiencing abuse, it is difficult to maintain stable emotions. Your emotions are more likely to be driven by your primitive survival instincts, rather than being able to use your mind to manage your emotional responses. This means you experience sudden and intense feelings of a range of emotions, such as anxiety, rage, fear, despair, sadness, or irritability, in response to the abuse or the uncertainty of abuse.

Like the single incident dilemma, where we lose the significance of abuse if we don't consider the context of the entire relationship, we also have to consider dysregulated emotions in the context of the abusive dynamic. The abuser's erratic behaviour is intensified by a range of factors, including the power imbalance, shifting blame, and their unhealthy belief system. These factors become a driving force behind the abuse and weaponize displays of erratic emotions. The survivor's dysregulated emotions are a direct response to experiencing abuse in the current situation and can further exacerbate the effects of it because of the power imbalance.

Although you might continue to feel dysregulated after abuse, there are coping skills and self-soothing tools you can learn to regulate your emotions.

Hypervigilance

Hypervigilance is a trauma response where you continuously assess the environment for threat, as there is a constant anticipation of danger. Tension building behaviours can lead to us developing a hyper awareness of subtle changes in the abuser's behaviour and our environment. We try to think five steps ahead, attempting to guess or anticipate the abuser's mood, or we feel as though we are walking on eggshells.

Hypervigilance is an attempt to self-protect by anticipating and preparing yourself for the threat of abuse. You try to anticipate what is going to trigger the abuser and seek to avoid it, to avoid being subjected to their criticism, insults, or their unpredictable mood. This leads to constantly searching to 'get it right'.

It can be exhausting in an environment where there is no consistency in what 'getting it right' actually means. This in part explains the mental exhaustion you may have felt in the relationship, because your mind works in overtime to assess your surroundings to keep you safe. It is in a near constant state of high alert, not having the opportunity for much needed periods of mental rest.

More than this, the notion of triggering the abuser can also lead to self-blame, as it places responsibility for their behaviour on your actions, when in fact their behaviour is driven by the central issues of power and control.

Low Self-Esteem

Tension building behaviours affect your self-esteem because not only is there no opportunity to develop a healthy attitude towards yourself, but the behaviours also *specifically target your attitude* towards yourself.

We can describe tension building behaviours as a siege on your self-worth. A siege is defined as a military operation, where the enemy surrounds a town to cut off essential supplies and compel those inside to surrender.

Tension building behaviours are an operation in which the abuser surrounds you with continuous negative input about self. They cut off essential positive input from your relationship with them, from others and eventually, even positive self-talk. The aim is to lower your self-esteem, to compel you to surrender to their position of power in the relationship.

In an unpredictable environment where we are criticised, devalued, invalidated, and blamed, the negative input becomes internalised. Our sense of self-worth is deeply affected, which can harm our mental health and lead to conditions such as anxiety or depression.

This is a contributing factor to why you feel at rock bottom during the abusive relationship or in the aftermath. It can feel as though the abuser has stripped you to your core and you have to build steadily and intently to regain a sense of self. *A sense of self that you care about.* Never mind full on self-love, the initial steps are all about just waking up and thinking to yourself, 'deep breath, I'm ok'. Recognising the abusive narrative you have internalised and saying, 'they are not my words', and finding small ways to increase self-worth through your day. This can be as simple as showing yourself small acts of kindness, such as allowing yourself to rest.

Self-Abandonment

Tension building behaviours condition you to forgo your own needs in favour of the abuser's. To avoid these types of abusive behaviours, bit by bit you might give up on expressing yourself. You stop having opinions, dressing the way you want to, trying to achieve your personal goals, or feeling as though you matter. There isn't any kind of mutual presence in the relationship. The entire relationship becomes centred on the abuser, the household revolving around anticipating their every mood and trying to appease and accommodate them.

From the abuser's perspective, if you aren't a separate person, then you are easier to control. If they feel they are always in the right, it's easier when you never disagree with them, rather than having to convince you. If they feel their needs are superior, then it is easier if you have given up on your needs, so they do not have to consider them. Or if they have a fragile ego, it is easier if they are in an environment where their ego isn't threatened by having to consider the needs and inherent worth of another.

In terms of a response to abuse, self-abandonment is an attempt to protect yourself from further negative input. If they heavily focused the abuse on parts of who you are, then it is a logical process that you attempt to avoid further abuse by abandoning those parts. Survivors of abuse often describe feeling a complete loss of self, and how they tried to remain invisible in the relationship. Or how they were invisible, and now struggle to identify who they are separate from the abuser.

You may feel shame for abandoning yourself, but if you understand it was self-protection, it can help ease the shame.

Self-abandonment presents in different ways, such as people pleasing, perfectionism, or self-criticism. These are based on prioritising the needs and judgement of others over your own and seeking validation through their approval. We hold ourselves to unrealistic expectations in order to achieve approval and not risk the threat of 'underperforming'. We learn to suppress our own needs, feelings, and values. It is when you honour these parts of yourself and recognise you are worthy, you can move away from the abusive narratives of tension building behaviours and increase self-worth.

Your intuition, needs, feelings and values deserve to be acknowledged.

5 ways to support your self-worth:

○ **Positive Self-Talk:** when you notice yourself being self-critical, mindfully (with intention) rephrase the statement to show more self-compassion. For example, 'I am always messing up', becomes 'I am human, I am doing the best I can'.

○ **Mindfulness:** mindfulness, yoga, meditation, or exercise can all help with regulating emotions and feeling less overwhelmed by powerful emotions.

○ **A Safe Environment:** we reduce hypervigilance by creating a safe space. Notice what helps you to feel safe or what triggers you in your environment. Try to make changes accordingly.

○ **Invest in Yourself:** build self-esteem by investing some time into yourself. You are acknowledging you are worthy of your time, and if you decide to develop a hobby or meet with friends, it also increases confidence.

○ **Affirmations:** start a journal to identify ways you may have self-abandoned. Then, respond with an affirmation. You can begin with gentle affirmations such as, 'I am not selfish to prioritise my needs', or 'I do not need to be perfect to be worthy of love'.

Chapter five:

Acute Pressure

We can characterise acute pressure as abuse that is not experienced on a day-to-day basis, although it may be an escalated version of day-to-day abuse. For example, criticism escalates to yelling, swearing, and throwing objects, or dismissive behaviour escalates to ceasing to communicate altogether. The fact it differs from the everyday abuse experienced, and it is commonly an escalated form of abuse, means the uncertainty and intensity of it creates an acute sense of pressure, anxiety, or urgency.

Emotional and psychological abusers are insidious with their forms of release. This is evident in the subtle abuse of the tension building behaviours. During escalated incidents, rather than an overt display of abuse, such as physical abuse or an explosion of rage, they may continue to abuse covertly through the form of goading you until you lose your temper. They then shame you and play the victim. Or they simply pull back from the relationship with no explanation of the sudden emotional withdrawal, triggering an intense fear of abandonment and attempts to regain their approval.

Acute Pressure Behaviours

Acute pressure behaviours are used with the desire to regain power and control through one of two aspects: intimidation or shame. The purpose of this is to mould and regulate your behaviour. These are powerful methods. If you don't respond to one, you will probably respond to the other. The reason for this is both intimidation and shame harness the element of fear.

Through intensified behaviour and uncertainty of the outcome, there is an acute lack of safety. There is uncertainty whether the abuser will ever 'return to normal', or whether they will end the relationship. There is fear whether they will spread lies about you or act upon any threats they have made. This can cause significant distress. You may experience them doing any of these things, or something else you find equally upsetting. This leads to acute pressure, a surge of panic, and scrambling to regain a sense of stability. Although still abusive, we would rather return to the day-to-day behaviours we are familiar with than experience the escalated abuse with its uncertain outcome.

When we think about our physical needs, such as water, food, and shelter, making our home environment unsafe is taking one of them away: a safe place to live. When your basic physical needs are not being met, you cannot flourish. When you do not have a feeling of safety in your home or relationship, it prevents you from being able to thrive. You cannot thrive in an environment which is harmful to you. It is this unhealthy environment and fear that keep you in a position of being controlled.

Aggressive Behaviour

- Rage (explosive or under the surface)
- Verbal abuse
- Physical intimidation
- Sexual aggression
- Swearing
- Yelling
- Throwing objects
- Restricting your free movement within the home

Aggressive behaviours create acute pressure through the abuser becoming a larger intimidating presence. It is an aggressive display of the power imbalance. The abuser uses their physical presence, including the tone and volume of their voice, to remind you of the relationship dynamic. The goal is to control the outcome of the situation by intimidating you into submission. This intimidation can incorporate elements of shame through their choice of words or by taking away your power by their physical presence.

Aggressive behaviours utilise the element of shock. The incident is sudden and unexpected. The door closes and WHAM... so many swear words, it doesn't even make sense. The volume is loud; the intensity is loud, the body language invasive, the verbal attack aggressive. All these elements are tapping into the shock factor, so you are stunned into submission through disbelief, panic, fear and confusion.

Aggressive behaviours also utilise unpredictability, often catching you off guard, which intensifies the panic and lack of safety. As well as trying to cope with their behaviour, you are trying to process what's happening, why it's happening and where the sudden attack has come from. The element of unpredictability means you are less able to prepare and protect yourself against the aggressive behaviours, as there is an overload of information to process whilst simultaneously having your survival responses activated.

Neglectful Behaviour

- Silent treatment
- Withholding affection
- Disregard or contempt towards your feelings, achievements and need for affection.
- Ignoring, intimidating, humiliating, or isolating you
- Preventing you from having basic needs met (such as food, clothing, or medical needs)

Neglect is a pattern of failing to meet essential needs in the relationship. Acute episodes of neglectful behaviours create pressure by pinpointing a basic need and withholding it, highlighting within us an urgency to have our need met and causing distress. The abuser escalates these forms of neglect to use them as punishment. We fear the loss of the abuser's approval and attention and feel a sense of panic as it may last indefinitely. This creates an acute sense of pressure to 'correct' our behaviour to appease the abuser and restore normality.

When it centres on emotional neglect, the abuser may refuse to communicate with you for an indefinite period. They completely ignore you, refusing to make eye contact or acknowledge your existence. Commonly referred to as the silent treatment, this is silent abuse and extremely painful. Research shows it activates the same parts of the brain as physical pain as it threatens psychological needs, such as belonging, self-esteem, and the ability to maintain safety in your environment.

Neglect also intensifies fear. Not only is there fear of the incident, but it triggers fears of abandonment, unworthiness, and helplessness. We feel completely at the mercy of the abuser in this moment. There is no security in the relationship, so when there is an acute episode of neglect, such as the silent treatment or humiliating you, the whole relationship comes into question. You cannot prepare yourself mentally for when they will communicate with you again, if they will 'forgive' you, or if they will leave you forever. As it invalidates our feelings and existence, we begin to feel inherently flawed. We might experience discomfort expressing feelings, as our needs are continuously neglected and used as a tool to control us.

This is a powerful reminder of the power imbalance. It acts as a reset button for the abuser, to make it clear who has the power and control.

Provoking Behaviour

- Shaming you
- Teasing disguised as 'a joke'
- Using your vulnerabilities against you
- Veiled threats (also aggression)
- Dog whistling (abuse / threats that only you can pick up on)

Provoking behaviours create acute pressure by tapping into your vulnerabilities and using them against you. The abuser learns what behaviours you would be ashamed of or who you are afraid of becoming. They learn when you feel you aren't good enough, what you are afraid of losing, and what triggers your feelings of fear and lack of safety. They then use this information to provoke a heightened emotional reaction from you.

The abusive incident doesn't always look like an explosive rage or manipulative silence. It can also be a measured attempt to provoke a reaction in you, so you are the one having an outburst. These behaviours are baiting you by triggering feelings such as fear, distress, shame, anger or a lack of safety. When you react, the abuser flips the script and uses your reaction as evidence you are abusive and unstable. They then claim your behaviour is the problem and blame you for the tensions in the relationship. This is a form of psychological abuse.

Provoking behaviours can leave us feeling unsafe within ourselves. We don't recognise ourselves or the way we are behaving. This leads to us having a greater loss of self-identity and relying even further on the abuser's reality, believing we are the unpredictable or abusive one. It is a manufactured situation, so you believe your behaviour is the issue and you are to blame, when the reality is, you are having a reaction to being abused.

Untangling Self (Pressure)

A common concern for survivors is the similarity between the silent treatment and how they themselves have withdrawn during incidents in the relationship. Survivors withdraw and shut down, as they have learned attempts to communicate are met with more abuse. Your silence is an attempt to protect yourself from further abuse in a hostile situation. This differs from the use of silence as abuse. The abuser perceives a threat of loss of control, but they use silence to punish you and emphasise the power imbalance. Your silence is a breakdown in healthy communication, but when attempts of healthy communication are met with further abuse, you can understand why you made this adaptation. Not to punish or control, but to survive.

The fear that develops from acute abuse can remain long after the incident. There is fear for safety, fear of being yourself, fear of upsetting the abuser, and fear of consequences. When you are living in fear of the abuser, it tips the balance of power firmly in their favour. People don't understand how you can be physically afraid of someone who wasn't physically violent towards you. But psychological abuse is built upon fear and the feeling the abuser can suffocate your existence if they choose to. It leaves you terrified at just the thought of being near them.

Survival Mode

When you are under physical or psychological threat, your nervous system responds by making physiological changes to help protect you from harm. We know this as the fight-flight response. This understanding has developed to include the freeze and fawn responses. You may experience symptoms such as sharpened visual and auditory senses, increased heart rate, quicker breathing, muscle tension and the release of adrenaline. There are also psychological changes, such as racing thoughts or a shift of focus onto the threat. These changes ready us for the perceived danger and optimise our chances of survival.

We often attach shame to how we respond to abuse. If you are a fighter, you might yell or push back and then compare your behaviour to the abuser's. If you freeze, you may feel shame for not protecting yourself and feel that you allowed them to abuse you. These, however, are instinctual human responses. It is your nervous system shifting into survival mode to ready you for the threat. You are responding in a way you have learned previously helped you survive.

This is your form of self-protection.

Fight

The fight response is an attempt to protect yourself by attacking the source of the perceived or real threat. You are more likely to have a fight response if you had rage or bullying behaviour modelled to you as a child, or experienced shaming and aggression. The fight response includes shouting or throwing objects, starting fights when feeling overwhelmed, and feeling irritated and defensive.

Flight

The flight response is an attempt to self-protect by putting distance between yourself and the perceived or real threat. If you have learned that avoiding those who treated you unkindly was a good way to minimise the impact of their behaviour, you may find you respond in flight mode. This includes avoiding uncomfortable conversations and emotions, perfectionistic tendencies to avoid criticism, and feeling restless, nervous, and confused.

Freeze

The freeze response is an attempt to self-protect by allowing yourself time to determine the best way to safeguard against the perceived or real threat. If you have experienced a continuation of abuse after attempting to protect yourself, you may find you respond in freeze mode as you unconsciously pause to assess how to manage the situation to minimise harm. This includes difficulty making decisions, daydreaming about escaping difficult situations and relationships, and feeling detached and numb.

Fawn

The fawn response is an attempt to protect yourself by appeasing the source of the perceived or real threat. You are more likely to have a fawning response if you have learned pleasing and accommodating others helped you to minimise harm. This includes forgoing your own needs and prioritising others, not having a strong sense of identity, and feeling shame and vulnerability.

Bessel Van Der Kolk discusses in his book, The Body Keeps the Score, how being able to take action to protect yourself from danger is critical in determining whether the negative experience will have a long-lasting effect. When you have been trapped in an abusive relationship, you have been living in survival mode, where you cannot protect yourself from the threat. This can lead to your acute stress response being triggered when it isn't needed, as you have developed a heightened sense of danger. You may have sudden displays of anger or uncontrollable tears over minor challenges in your day (fight). There may be a feeling of anxiety unless you know every detail of plans, so you can cancel if you feel unsafe (flight). You may feel numb towards making decisions or making social connections (freeze). Or you may feel unworthy unless you prioritise the needs of others over your own (fawn).

If you've ever been told to get over it, let go, move on, or it happened so long ago, understanding the stress responses can help ease the shame of these expectations. You respond to past abuse in current situations because your nervous system is automatically jumping into action to keep you safe. You are not living in the past; you are living in the present and healing the effects of past abuse.

Reactive Abuse

Reactive abuse is your fight mode being activated in response to abuse. When you are being abused, you try to defend yourself through lashing out, verbal insults, or even physically. The abuser may even provoke you until you snap. They then use your fight response to further blame you for the hostile relationship and claim they are the victim. Reactive abuse is hard to process as it causes confusion and shame over your own behaviour and a genuine fear that you are abusive yourself. Due to the abuser's manipulation of how you have reacted, it can also make it difficult to access support. Where the abuse is measured and happens behind closed doors, the response is reactive and not so easily contained. You might react to abuse in public. The abuser then manipulates the perception of others to reduce the significance of their abusive behaviour and draw attention to your reaction.

They utilise the appearance of remaining calm whilst you appear to 'attack' them.

Psychotherapist Pete Walker describes how being trapped in the fight response can lead to abusive tendencies; in other words, *some abusers are stuck in fight mode*. For example, the abuser unconsciously believes they can receive the love and safety they did not receive as a child through their power and control over others. They inflict abuse and hold power over how they receive love by controlling their relationships, to no longer be the victim or feel neglected. Their fight mode is over-engaged, and this explains why, if you respond to abuse in fight mode, you notice similarities between your behaviour and the abuser's.

This does not make you 'just as abusive' towards the abuser, however.

The term reactive abuse implies a level of equality in the relationship that just isn't there. In the abusive relationship, there is a major power imbalance. Although your behaviour may be reactive, it is not on a par with the abuse. The abuser is yelling and attacking from a position of power and control. The survivor is yelling and defending from a position of minimal power and control. In what other situation, when a victim is under attack, do we label their response a 'reactive attack'? We don't. We call it self-defence.

Stress Toll

A survivor told me how she was diagnosed with Crohn's disease two years before meeting her abusive boyfriend, and her Crohn's was under control with medication. Within 6 months of dating the abuser, she was hospitalised with a flare up. Their relationship lasted ten years, and over that time, she was hospitalised at least once a year because of her Crohn's. She developed bulimia and at one point was having binging and purging episodes at least three times a day, throwing up approximately 20-30 times daily. She also experienced episodes of intense heart palpitations.

Although they are now separated, she still has periods of significant stress with the abuser, as they have a child together. Although at times, she feels this is more stressful than the relationship itself, her health improvements would suggest otherwise. In the ten years since they separated, she has never been hospitalised for Crohn's, only experiencing mild symptoms. She has a healthier relationship with food and is no longer binging or purging, and her heart palpitations have stopped completely. Notably, although there are periods of heightened stress, she is no longer living in an environment of *continuous stress.*

Although the stress she still goes through can feel overwhelming, the difference is it is not a constant fixture in her environment. Stress is a known contributor and aggravator to various health issues. We know it adversely affects the immune system, digestive system, and cardiovascular system. It also affects your mood, such as feeling fatigued, irritable, or finding it difficult to concentrate. Stress may also be an underlying cause of other diseases, as, if we adopt unhealthy ways to cope, this will have a negative impact on our health. The body is built to cope with short bursts of stress effectively, even if they are intense. It is not built to respond continuously to threat, which is why a constant stressor, such as living with an abuser, has an accumulative negative effect on physical and mental wellbeing.

5 ways to regulate your nervous system:

- o **Self-Regulation:** breathing exercises, crying, physical activity, going for a walk, or cold sensations (a cold shower or dunking your face in cold water) helps to regulate your nervous system and you can do it alone.
- o **Co-Regulation:** connecting with others, such as breathing exercises together, or calling someone you trust, physical touch, such as hugging or laughing with a friend, provides support in calming your nervous system's response.
- o **Learn what situations trigger you to feel unsafe...** but also, *in what situations do you feel safe?* This helps to establish coping strategies and to incorporate things that provide safety into your environment.
- o **Learn what emotions trigger your stress response:** feeling unheard, abandoned, powerless, unworthy? This helps you to identify the origin of your stress response, to give yourself compassion and to work on these emotional triggers.
- o **Is the threat perceived or real?** Identifying if the threat is perceived or real helps you to establish what action you can take to cope. Whether to step back and use the tools you have gained to self-soothe, or whether action needs to be taken to protect yourself.

Chapter six:

Manipulation

Abusers use a range of manipulative tactics to avoid accountability for their behaviour, shift blame and keep you confused about the reality of abuse. This is to keep you invested in the relationship, and to manipulate the outcome of your interactions, therefore maintaining power and control. Manipulation intensifies directly after experiencing incidents of acute pressure or overt episodes of abuse, as the abuser must work harder to justify and avoid accountability for escalated incidents. However, like the micro patterns of abuse, subtle manipulation also runs as an undercurrent throughout the relationship to undermine your feelings and influence your perception, behaviour, and decision making on a daily basis.

Manipulative Behaviours

We experience so much self-doubt during the abusive relationship by design. It is a form of psychological programming to make you doubt yourself, which is achieved through a variety of manipulative tactics. There is a misconception that abusers only target people with low self-esteem. Some are opportunist and others see confident people as a challenge. What they do, however, is target your self-esteem during the relationship, and one way to do this is to create a lack of self-trust through manipulation. This leads to chronic self-doubt and reduced self-esteem. It's hard to remain confident when you constantly question yourself. This means you are more reliant on the abuser's reality, which is how the abuser uses manipulation to establish power and control.

The confusion and doubt keep you stuck trying to process whether their behaviour is acceptable or whether yours is not. If you had more clarity, you would not tolerate their abuse. You would take action to change the relationship dynamic, whether that be trying to communicate with them about their abusive behaviour or deciding to leave. The primary aim of manipulation is for the abuser to avoid accountability so they can continue with their controlling behaviour. The primary target of manipulation is to make you question your perception, judgement and intuition. This is so you become so consumed with doubt you will accept the abuser's version of reality as your own and, therefore, will 'accept' how they treat you.

Manipulative behaviours keep you focused on your own behaviour and the validity of your thoughts and feelings, not allowing you the time or mental capacity to recognise the abuse and hold the abuser accountable.

Guilt

When we feel guilty, it is because we feel uncomfortable with an aspect of our choices or our actions. One way we look to relieve guilt is to handle it differently the next time we face a similar situation.

An abuser creates guilt over reasonable choices and healthy boundaries to manipulate you into handling the situation differently. The guilt leads to you feeling uncomfortable with your reasonable choice, and the manipulation causes you to question whether it was in fact reasonable. To relieve this discomfort, you make changes when you face a similar situation. Because of the self-doubt being fostered by using guilt to manipulate you, you are inclined to trust the abuser's version of what is reasonable. This means your actions fall in line with what the abuser wants from you, rather than what would be a healthy and reasonable choice for yourself.

One survivor's story is an example of how guilt was used to manipulate her into withdrawing from her friends and family. When she first started dating her boyfriend, she had a strong social group and lived close to her family. She also had a young son. Her boyfriend grew up in a different neighbourhood, so did not have any friends or family nearby. When they moved in together, he told her she was inconsiderate to meet her friends as this meant he was always left alone. She just left him alone, without a thought, whilst she went out and had fun. He told her she was selfish because she was using him as a babysitter. When she told him her mother could look after her son, he refused and shifted focus by accusing her of believing he was incapable of looking after her child. He also questioned her loyalty to him and even her own son, stating it was clear where her priorities lay, even if she couldn't see it.

This manipulative behaviour triggered immense feelings of guilt. She felt uncomfortable to socialise with her friends because she felt she was choosing to be a bad girlfriend and mother. She questioned whether she was, in fact, being inconsiderate towards the two people she cared most about, which led to her meeting with her friends less and less frequently. The abuser (her boyfriend) created an environment where she was manipulated into forgoing her own needs, questioning whether it was even reasonable for her to have social needs. After not seeing her friends for some time, she said to the abuser she might try to see them again. His response was, 'I doubt they would want to meet up with you after you ditched them. You are not a great friend'.

She felt such shame and guilt she didn't contact her friends again until after the relationship was over. Five years later.

Triangulation

Triangulation brings a third person into the relationship to manipulate the opinions and behaviour of those involved and to maintain control. The abuser is the pivotal point of contact, where everyone relies on them for communicating with one another. We often see this with an abusive parent, where they compare siblings favourably or unfavourably to one another, which triggers competition and a need to perform, either to remain in favour or to gain approval.

For adult siblings, the abusive parent becomes the hub of information for family plans, with minimal communication directly between siblings. The abuser uses this position to stir animosity, conflict, and jealousy. They tell you, 'your brother has spoken poorly of you' or 'your sister feels hard done by', or 'the family feels you haven't contributed to the plans enough'. The abusive parent talks in private to each member of the family and feigns understanding and camaraderie, the 'us against them' mentality, to create friction between all siblings and ensure they maintain a central position of control.

Think, divide and conquer.

Abusers also triangulate with past relationships. The abuser compares you to someone from their past, saying, 'my ex never had this issue', or 'why can't you just be more like...'. This keeps your self-esteem low and feeling as though you can never live up to their expectations BUT believing their expectations are achievable because someone else lived up to them. The issue here is, you believe you are the problem, not the abusive behaviour, which is how triangulation works to manipulate you into trying harder to please them. Conversely, the abuser compares you favourably to others, which creates pressure for you to continue to perform and meet their expectations, so that you don't become another one of their 'crazy exes'. The comparisons, however, are likely either fully fabricated, based on half-truths or are a distorted reality of the abuser, omitting the fact their abuse elicited the responses from previous relationships which led to others being labelled as crazy.

Fake Emotions

We have already discussed how abusers use anger to intimidate. Even though abusers appear to have an issue with anger management, research suggests they are in control of their anger and are choosing to display it as a tool to achieve their desired outcome. This is manipulation.

Displays of fake emotions to manipulate are not limited to anger. When the abuser perceives they are losing control, they resort to big displays of emotions. They show anger, sobbing, distress, or disgust. This undermines your position through intimidation, shame or appealing to your empathy. They aim to manipulate the outcome of the situation through these emotive performances. One survivor discussed how she had never seen her partner cry throughout their marriage. At the breakdown of their marriage, he went to the bathroom and cried in the 'loudest, most alarming way'. He had already tried various ways to re-establish the dynamic but had failed. After several minutes, he calmly returned and asked if she had heard him crying, looking as though he had never shed a tear. When she replied she had and it was evident to him his effort to manipulate her was ineffective, he moved onto the next tactic to regain control, and stonewalled her (refused to communicate) for the following week.

Gaslighting

Gaslighting is a form of psychological abuse. It is a type of manipulation which undermines your reality and is used to create a power imbalance through distorting your thoughts, causing confusion, invalidating your emotions and denying your experiences. It has a long-lasting impact on your wellbeing, leading to chronic self-doubt, intense confusion, distress, low self-esteem, and loss of identity.

The aim of gaslighting is to control the relationship dynamic and avoid accountability for their behaviour. The abuser achieves this through tactics which cause you to question your perception, memories and intuition, so you are so consumed with doubt you accept the abuser's version of reality as your own. The abuser manipulates the truth so that you doubt your understanding of the situation, which allows them to continue with their abusive behaviour and maintain power and control.

Gaslighting behaviours include:

Denial

Denial is where the abuser outright denies the event happened and says things like you're crazy or a liar. When you have a clear memory of the event which is being so adamantly denied, it can feel crazy making, so you believe the only logical explanation must be your perception is incorrect.

Minimising

The abuser says you're too sensitive, always overreacting or it was no big deal. This is minimising the abusive behaviour and shifting fault onto your valid reaction rather than taking accountability.

Countering

Countering is where the abuser will bring up your perceived wrong doings or behaviour to 'counter argue' the inappropriateness of their own behaviour. They say things like you never remember things accurately, or you raise your voice more often than they do, bringing focus to your 'flaws' or your reaction instead of acknowledging their abusive behaviour.

Withholding

Withholding is the refusal to talk about what happened or any deeper issues until you give up and just let it go, so they can avoid accountability. The abuser pretends they don't understand, or says you are trying to confuse them. They also withhold affection or warmth until you give up on trying to receive an apology or resolving the issue.

Blame

The abuser often places blame on the victim, but they also blame life stressors or other people for their abusive behaviour. Work is stressful, life is stressful, they have a lot on their plate, they haven't been well, and you should be more understanding. You then question your behaviour rather than holding the abuser accountable. It leads to feelings of shame and not feeling good enough in the relationship.

Untangling Self (Manipulation)

These processes are similar to common unconscious defence mechanisms that many of us engage in, to some extent. We might deny, minimise, and rationalise our behaviour or choices. We do this when we feel vulnerable about ourselves and holding ourselves accountable for our actions or behaviour can feel overwhelming, so we avoid it. Maybe you have told a white lie or became defensive when someone called you out on your behaviour. However, we also want to treat people with fairness, not to harm others, and to abide by our own morals and values. This moral component often leads to self-reflection and the ability to consider the other person's perspective, as well as identify where we are avoiding accountability for ourselves. We want to repair relationships when there is conflict, which is part of what drives us to consider the other person's perspective and adjust.

The abuser engages in manipulative behaviour to avoid accountability, with little to no consideration of your perspective. They are driven by a need to self-protect and self-serve. Rather than repair, the overriding focus is control of the situation. They either lack the moral component or the stage of self-reflection. Therefore, they continue to engage in manipulative behaviours, to avoid accountability and maintain power and control, even though it can cause you significant psychological harm.

Manipulation has a spiralling effect. It is both the cause of and intensified by:

Loss of Self-Trust

At the core of self-doubt is a loss of self-trust. When you lose a sense of self-trust, self-doubt grows, and this leads to feeling mentally 'foggy'. Mental fog can cause heaviness and exhaustion when you try to gain clarity of your own experiences, as if trying to reach a sound conclusion is a mental exercise in climbing Mount Everest. The mind struggles to make sense of conflicting stimuli; your experiences versus the information (from the abuser) about those experiences. Or your feelings versus how you are told you should feel. Your mind is working overtime. Reality becomes shrouded in confusion, and it is difficult to determine the truth.

Without self-trust in your own thoughts and judgement, you may doubt your sanity. The heavier the mental fog, the more unstable you feel, and this supports the false narrative that you are the unstable one in the relationship. This is something the abuser uses to their advantage. Through further manipulation, they encourage a feeling of instability and may encourage others to see you as unstable as well. This not only makes you even more dependent on their distorted reality, but it is a great way to avoid present and future accountability. The abuser has already set the scene where you and others view yourself as irrational.

Detachment

Dissociation is a form of self-protection, whereby you detach from your feelings, thoughts, or surroundings to cope with high levels of stress after trauma. It feels like you're in a bubble, or everyone around you is in the Truman Show and you're playing a role, watching them as though you aren't really a part of it. You are physically there but mentally numb. However, after chronic gaslighting, we may also detach from connecting with others because we lose self-trust in reading social situations. This can cause you to feel detached from your relationships.

The effects of gaslighting mean you question your perception of other people's intentions, whether they are trustworthy, and whether you can trust your understanding of who they are and the relationship. This leads to you not only having difficulty in connecting, but also avoiding emotional connection, to protect yourself from being hurt again. When you break it down, this is a logical response. If you were persistently told you misread the abuser and didn't communicate yourself well, socialising, maintaining, and forming new relationships can feel immensely overwhelming.

The issue with detaching from others is it amplifies the voice of manipulation. When we connect in safe relationships, we experience interacting with another and seeing their intentions are genuine. We experience socialising and noticing how someone's body language and mood correspond and build evidence we can read the situation correctly. We experience the ease of conversation when someone isn't trying to trip us up or undermine us at every opportunity. We connect with someone who is mutually engaged in honest communication.

These experiences help to build self-trust. And as you build self-trust, and greater self-awareness, the manipulation loses power.

Self-Gaslighting

There are two common elements to self-gaslighting that you may have experienced.

First, when we invalidate our own responses. We deny, minimise, and blame ourselves for the abuse. This extends the abusive narrative, where you have internalised the message that it's all in your head (deny), you are just too sensitive (minimise) and they are only abusive because of something you have done (blame). It is also a form of self-protection. Acknowledging the extent of abuse can be overwhelming, especially if you are in a position where you feel trapped and unable to protect yourself. So, your mind protects you by not acknowledging the extent of it. However, this unintentionally invalidates the response you have to abuse.

The second is when we do not accept ourselves or the situation. This is more appropriately described as a defence mechanism, to protect ourselves from the enormity of abuse and internalising blame. You may feel over-responsible for others and concerned with behaving 'correctly'. When you fall short of these unrealistic standards, you deny, minimise and struggle to accept your actions because you have learned anything other than perfect standards of behaviour warrants being abused. Survivors struggle with accepting their choices because it is implied they somehow contributed to the abuse.

You feel you must be perfect to not be complicit *in being abused.*

This leads to deep shame because none of us are perfect. People will not even agree on the perfect way to respond in a given situation. Just because you don't 'behave perfectly' all the time does not mean you deserved abuse, or that you contributed to being abused. Part of growth is allowing yourself to make choices, *and mistakes,* whilst remaining constant in your understanding that your choices and mistakes do not cause or warrant abuse from others.

What Isn't Gaslighting

Many phrases the abuser uses to gaslight you are the same as you genuinely feel about them. This means the language used by you and the abuser may be similar. When you are experiencing a high level of self-doubt (because of gaslighting!), the similarity in language perpetuates feelings of confusion, doubt, and distress (which are all effects of gaslighting!).

Even if it seems the same on the surface, it is not the same. The abuser says it to manipulate, whereas you say it as an accurate description of the situation.

This can sound like:

"That never happened"

Gaslighting: said to deny something that you (and they) have a clear memory of.

Accurate: said to the abuser when they accuse you of something you didn't do (sometimes projecting their own behaviour).

"You're not making any sense"

Gaslighting: said even though they understand you.

Accurate: said to the abuser (or thought to yourself) when they communicate in a way to create confusion.

"You're overreacting"

Gaslighting: said when you have a reasonable emotional response to their behaviour.

Accurate: said (or thought) when the abuser shows volatile or aggressive behaviour towards you, often to defend yourself and attempt to diffuse their behaviour, not to manipulate.

Differences of opinion, or the occasional insensitive or inconsiderate response, does not mean you or someone else is gaslighting. Gaslighting is a pattern of denying your experiences. Like with many covert abusive behaviours, it's difficult to distinguish when it is happening. Remember, psychological abuse targets the way you think, to distort your reality and foster self-doubt.

Signs You've Experienced Gaslighting

- Confusion and doubt
- Difficulty making decisions
- Loss of confidence
- Feeling nervous that you misunderstood, or your feelings are wrong
- Questioning whether you're 'crazy' or 'too sensitive'
- Feeling undermined
- When you raise issues, the conversation often ends up about you
- Overly apologetic
- Unhappy (but don't know why)
- Feeling afraid (but don't know why)
- Making excuses for their behaviour

A consequence of gaslighting is having a thought or feeling and being disconnected from the reason. This is because manipulative behaviour has invalidated your reason for feeling the way you do. You struggle to accept how you feel, believing you should feel something else. For example, feeling like you should apologise although you don't know what you've done wrong. Feeling unhappy, but you don't believe you have anything to be unhappy about. Feeling afraid but not understanding why. Or making excuses for their behaviour, although you're unsure if they're behaving reasonably.

Holding awareness of manipulative behaviours will help you identify them more clearly and take a step back. More than this, however, is learning to separate someone else's understanding of you from your understanding of yourself. When you are reliant on the abuser's opinion of you, you are deeply affected by it. This means, when they show disappointment in you, when they say you've overreacted, or they say you have behaved unfairly, you internalise it. Their opinion of you becomes your opinion of you. Their manipulation becomes what you believe. This can extend to others, where we form our understanding of ourselves based on the opinion of those around us.

Through gaining a clearer understanding of yourself, you become less concerned with how others perceive you and, therefore, less affected by what they think of you. Just because someone is disappointed in your choice doesn't mean it was the wrong decision for you. Just because someone feels you should have handled it differently doesn't mean you didn't handle it in the best way for your circumstances. And just because someone says it's no big deal, doesn't mean you should deny the significance of the experience to yourself.

5 ways to overcome manipulative behaviour:

o **Limit contact** with the person / people who gaslight you as much as possible. With distance, it is easier to identify their behaviour and gain a stronger sense of self.

o **Keep a brief log** of communication for you to refer to, so you have a source of reference (and clarity) if they try to alter how the conversation proceeded. This is not to convince the abuser; this is for yourself.

o **Remind yourself** you do not have to defend or justify your perception, thoughts, and feelings. Instead, affirm to yourself your experiences were real, you know what you experienced, and your thoughts and feelings are valid.

o **Face the Inner Critic:** asking questions like, 'where does it come from', and 'what role does it have?' can help to build self-trust by understanding your inner critic. Show yourself you can handle the situation, with responses such as, 'I recognise these are not my words', or 'I understand the inner critic is afraid of me taking a risk and failing, but I don't need to protect myself with harsh words'.

o **Self-Care:** show yourself you are trustworthy by setting aside time for yourself. Check in with yourself once a week to see if you have considered your needs, worked towards a goal, or allowed yourself time to rest.

Chapter seven:

Trauma Bonding

Trauma bonding is when you develop an emotional attachment to someone who is toxic or abusive towards you. In the cycle of abuse, I have renamed the Calm or Honeymoon phase Trauma Bonding, as the periods of calm and affectionate behaviours are an integral part of what creates and sustains the trauma bond. Along with the practical, financial, and social difficulties of leaving an abusive relationship, there is also the emotional attachment. This is the trauma bond, which can long outlast the relationship and cause substantial inner conflict.

The memories of 'honeymoon' behaviours play a significant role in the emotional attachment. However, the affectionate behaviours of the abuser aren't really a honeymoon phase to be looked upon fondly and to reminisce about, but a break from the abusive behaviours to reinforce the trauma bond and power imbalance. With a clear perspective, you can soothe the regret for what could have been. We often pine for the 'good times'. Yet, these memories are misleading. When you focus on them, they portray an image of calmness and kindness, and this builds a completely different understanding of the relationship than the reality. One that you deeply attach to. If you widen your scope, however, you will see these memories are the eye of the storm. A moment of calm in a relationship that is otherwise consistently abusive.

Trauma Bonding Behaviours

There are two key characteristics to a trauma bonded relationship: intermittent reinforcement and a power imbalance. The power imbalance creates the feeling of helplessness, where you feel as though you don't have any control over the outcome or direction of the relationship. The intermittent reinforcement, which provides you with moments of joy, affection and attention in an otherwise high stress environment, causes you to look to the abuser to soothe and comfort you. Even though they are also the source of your pain.

In combination, the power imbalance and intermittent reinforcement mean you lean further into the relationship. They intensify the trauma bond as you seek the abuser's affection to counter their abuse, becoming more deeply attached to the good times you have with them to soothe the pain, rejection and distress felt in the relationship.

Power Imbalance

The power imbalance is an essential factor in making us lean further into the abusive relationship to seek comfort. If there was a balance of power, treating you kindly after abuse would not have the same affect. The helplessness created by the power imbalance means you develop a dependency on the abuser. You might feel they have so much control over you and the relationship, you have no choice but to accept how they behave or cannot break free. You therefore become dependent on them as your source of comfort, joy, intimacy, and validation. If you leave the relationship, you might feel lost without them, because although you have lost the source of your pain, they were also the person you were dependent on to ease the pain.

Intermittent Reinforcement

Intermittent reinforcement is the acts of kindness scattered into the abusive relationship, which ultimately lead to a stronger attachment and seeking the abuser's affection and approval. It may be affection after a barrage of verbal abuse, or an extravagant day trip after an explosive rage. A gift, a compliment, or some recognition. The intermittent reinforcement may be random small acts of kindness throughout the week alongside abusive behaviours, or longer periods of affection, attention, and kindness where the abusive behaviour is minimal. Or, simply, respite from their abusive behaviour which provides a moment of calm.

A key element of intermittent reinforcement is it is unpredictable. The same behaviours from you won't always lead to kindness. Equally, the same abusive incidents won't always result in the same 'rewards' of affection, appreciation, or remorse. The uncertainty of when and how you will receive kindness results in you investing more to gain it. It is the same principle as a gambler at a slot machine; the uncertainty of when the next pay-out will come results in them becoming more emotionally invested in attempting to gain it. They invest more of their money, even though they could make huge losses whilst pursuing the unpredictable reward. Yet, they know from experience there is a possibility of winning, so they maintain hope. When you have previously experienced the abuser will eventually behave kindly towards you, it gives you hope to continue to try and appease them. This is coupled with the unpredictability of when it will happen, keeping you invested in trying to restore the good times for longer than you otherwise would.

It also reinforces the confusion and doubt over how you perceive the relationship and their behaviour. Intermittent good behaviour leads you to question whether you perceived the severity of their abusive behaviour correctly, or whether it really is all in your head. The sporadic acts of kindness strengthen the gaslighting narrative - that it is your perception causing the problem rather than the behaviour itself. Abusers even use their acts of kindness as evidence 'you're crazy' if you attempt to hold them accountable for their abuse.

Settling for Crumbs

Settling for crumbs is an aspect of intermittent reinforcement, whereby we become grateful to receive positive behaviour from the abuser, even though any positive behaviour from them is the bare minimum. The level of kindness is much less than anyone deserves to be treated with. Yet, we settle for the crumbs of affection.

When we look at the abusive dynamic, there has been the development of dependency and control as part of the cornerstones of abuse, the critical tension building behaviours and episodes of acute pressure. There is also increased uncertainty and a lack of security within yourself and your surroundings through manipulative behaviours. This lowers self-esteem and creates a sense of helplessness. It also creates an environment of high stress, where you will release higher levels of cortisol. These factors cause us to settle for much less than we deserve. We accept the bare minimum in terms of human respect, warmth and kindness in order to keep the peace, because we crave pleasure and calmness.

We can compare it to someone who is being starved of food. Their body and mind longs for the next meal, not knowing when it will come, but longing for it to be soon. When it finally comes, it is only a dried scrap of bread, but it's been so long since they've eaten anything, they are just grateful to have some food. It feels unbelievably good to eat, even though it is, in fact, only a stale piece of bread. They even allow themselves to hope it won't be so long until they eat again and experience the feeling of having a meal.

This is the same as the unhealthy bond. Except, instead of being starved of food, you are being starved of emotional warmth and connection. More than this, we feel as though we don't deserve more than the crumbs of kindness. The abuser places blame on us for the tensions and their negative behaviour. When we internalise this message, we feel as though they are showing us kindness simply by 'putting up' with us, and therefore feel grateful for the minimal warmth we receive.

Untangling Self (Trauma Bond)

The trauma bond is the continuation of a strong emotional attachment to the abuser, even though their behaviour is intolerable. You may see the behaviour is abusive or manipulative and yet the acts of kindness cloud your ability to make sense of your relationship and experiences. This leads to denying, minimising, or excusing the abuse. Their kindness provides pain relief, so you also block out the abusive behaviour, largely forget it and push it to the back of your mind, focusing on the positive behaviour instead, to cope with the hurt and abuse.

Survivors struggle with the inner conflict this creates, asking themselves why they still love or care for the abuser. It can lead to feelings of distress or shame. However, abuse is a painful experience, so naturally you block out the bad parts and focus on the good as protection from the pain. There is no shame in this. There's no shame in loving someone, and there's no shame in trying to protect yourself from the hurt they caused.

An Addictive Bond

Hormones also contribute to the strength of the trauma bond. The contrast between feeling high levels of stress and craving pleasure results in an addictive bond, which is biochemical, not just emotional. In an otherwise high stress environment, the abuser's positive behaviour serves as a reward and triggers the release of dopamine, giving you the sought after feeling of pleasure. This strengthens the trauma bond, as you seek to reduce stress and increase pleasure, by attempting to appease the abuser and gain their positive rewards of attention, affection, kindness and calm.

This results in a stronger attachment to the 'good times' in abusive relationships compared to healthy relationships, where respectful and caring behaviour is consistent. Due to the high stress environment and inconsistent positive behaviour, the pleasure felt during the good times is intensified, creating a much stronger attachment and desire for them. It can result in us feeling numb when we are not experiencing the highs and lows of such a volatile relationship.

It is partly why we feel devastated by the loss of the relationship, even though it was abusive. By interjecting the negative behaviour with some positive experiences, the abuser keeps the element of hope alive and builds a biochemical and emotional attachment. The good times have been magnified. It means you may actually experience symptoms of withdrawal from the abuser, like an addiction, where you crave the connection with them to soothe your stress levels and feel the pleasure of when they are kind.

There is nothing wrong with you if you miss them terribly, if you can't stop thinking about them and you feel you don't know how to function without them. So many survivors have reached out to me in visible pain, believing something is wrong with them because they still want to be with the abuser. You may be able to reason with yourself that it makes no sense, given how they treated you, but the emotional attachment runs much deeper.

There is nothing wrong with you. This feeling won't always be so intense.

Signs of Trauma Bonding

- You feel you cannot function without them, even though they give you little in terms of mutual love, respect, or compromise.
- You don't recognise them or yourself anymore, but still cannot leave the relationship.
- The relationship is filled with empty promises and inconsistencies.
- You have tried to leave but keep getting drawn back in by their apologies or grand gestures of change and affection.
- You feel deeply unhappy with them but still feel unable to break the bond.
- You feel protective of them, make excuses for their behaviour and focus on the 'good times'.
- You feel you gave up everything and did all you could to make them happy, but nothing is ever enough.
- High levels of stress present in other ways, such as through self-harm, addiction or affecting your mental health.

Recognising their good behaviour as part of the abusive relationship will support you in breaking the emotional attachment. Acknowledge the storm, not just the eye of the storm. This will support you in shifting focus onto your growth and away from reminiscing and regret over the relationship. Survivors of abuse often talk about the peace they experience in their day to day lives once they have moved beyond the initial pain and distress of separation.

We often feel deeply concerned whether we could have done more to make the relationship work. If you look at how much you have given, there is a likelihood you even gave up large parts of yourself. It's more than anyone should expect. You gave everything you could, and then some. You are not to blame for the abuse or the strong attachment. With distance and awareness, you are in a better position to show self-acceptance of your emotions and responses, which will support you in your growth and peace of mind.

5 ways to break the trauma bond:

o **Keep a journal** inclusive of abusive incidents: this will help you maintain a balanced perspective when the good times are intensified in your memory.

o **Acknowledge** the positive behaviour as part of the abusive dynamic, rather than focusing on the good times.

o **Recognise the trauma bond.** When you are aware of the strong emotional attachment, it helps you manage the powerful emotions connected to the relationship without being drawn back into it and without feeling shame.

o **Ask yourself,** would you want your relationship for a friend, inclusive of the good and bad times? It's easier to identify if a relationship is healthy by creating some distance.

o **Have as minimal contact as possible** with the abuser. This gives you the opportunity to grow without being subjected to either their abuse or their random acts of kindness.

SURVIVOR'S GUIDE
UNTANGLING SELF TAKEAWAYS:

· The four categories of abusive behaviour are: Building Tensions, Acute Pressure, Manipulation and Trauma Bonding. We may experience these cyclically, or they may be simultaneous.

· Tension building behaviours are critical, demeaning, and unpredictable which focus negatively on you, placing blame for the tension on your behaviour.

· Tension building behaviours can lead to feelings of hypervigilance, low self-esteem, internalising abuse and self-abandonment. We counter this by developing a compassionate inner voice.

· The abuser creates acute pressure through aggressive, neglectful, and provoking behaviour, which leads to a lack of safety.

· In response to acute pressure, you typically experience the fight, flight, freeze, or fawn response. Understanding your response helps you implement coping strategies and ease shame.

· Abusers use a range of manipulative tactics to avoid accountability for their behaviour, shift blame and keep you confused about the reality of abuse.

· We counter manipulation with clarity of manipulative behaviour and having an independent understanding of ourselves, rather than forming an opinion of ourselves based on how others perceive us. This enables you to recognise and be less affected by manipulation. Remaining firmer in the truth of your experiences.

· Trauma bonding is a strong emotional attachment to the abuser, which has two characteristics: intermittent reinforcement and a power imbalance.

· You are not to blame for abuse or the strong attachment. Recognising the good times as part of the abusive relationship will support you in accepting your emotions and breaking the trauma bond, helping you to gain peace of mind.

Untangling Self Affirmations

I am not to blame for...

My feelings of ....

....

are valid.

It is not an overreaction to feel...

I have a right to voice...

I have a right to feel upset by...

I can trust my perception of...

I give myself permission to feel...

Part Three

Potential versus Reality

One obstacle in restoring clarity is the contrast between who we believe the abuser to be and the reality of who they are. Accepting who they are is difficult, but before we even get to that point, is the difficulty in *understanding* who they are. So much doesn't match up. Words and actions. Who they are in public and at home. Who they were at the beginning and who they seem to become. Their unsightly behaviour, kept a hidden secret, is the polar opposite of the person you know them to be. Or you think them to be. Who other people see. *To their potential.*

People ask, 'why did you put up with it if it was so bad?' You may even ask yourself this question. Foremost, first impressions make a big impact; we become very attached to them. Research shows it takes just a tenth of a second to form an impression of someone, and this initial impression doesn't significantly change with longer exposure. If anything, it serves to boost our confidence in our initial judgement. Marketing also knows this. A good first impression creates a loyal customer even if your next products aren't as good.

What does this mean in an abusive relationship? Well, first impressions of the abuser make a lasting impact. This first impression forms a template of who you understand them to be. We all show our best behaviour when we are first getting to know someone, but the difference is, as the relationship progresses, and we show more of ourselves, it doesn't disrupt the template that was first formed about us. It expands the template of understanding who we are.

With an abuser, when their abusive behaviour shows, it destroys the template of who you understand them to be, formed by your first experiences with them. This means, instead of expanding on your understanding of who they are, you have to re-write it. This is a difficult task for anyone, not just someone who has been abused. Hence, we respond by searching for experiences and behaviours that support the original version of our understanding of them.

In some form, we disregard the abusive behaviour that makes no sense to us.

This is how you experience cognitive dissonance, where you have conflicting beliefs and thoughts about the abuser and your experiences. There is a disconnect between what you believe and what you are experiencing. The disconnect is intensified through the processes of idealisation, devaluation, and discard which form part of covert abusive relationships. Once again, rather than phases, I will explore them as sets of beliefs or attitudes that are idealising, devaluing or discarding you. This is because every survivor's experience is unique. Some experience these attitudes in a cyclical nature, whilst others experience them in different forms, such as one family member being idealised whilst the other is devalued, or where the attitudes seem to overlap or merge.

We also hold onto the abuser's potential. The potential is alluring for two reasons. First, the belief of who they are, or who they are when they are idealising us, often attends to our childhood wounds. If you felt unseen as a child, then when the abuser gives you excessive positive attentiveness, your inner child feels seen. Therefore, you form an emotional attachment to their potential, and giving up on their potential feels like a return to being invisible again.

Second, holding onto the abuser's potential can be a protective coping mechanism. Their potential gives hope, and feeling hope is soothing when experiencing abuse. It is less uncomfortable than acknowledging the reality of the relationship and, therefore, the pain of abuse. The irony is, holding onto their potential will amplify your inner wounds, because the abuser does not meet your needs, and the pain caused by the relationship long-term will outweigh the short-term pain of facing reality.

Cognitive dissonance creates inner conflict, such as stress, anxiety, regret, and sadness. We ask questions such as, 'how did the love of my life became the bully in my life?' Or 'how did someone who was so committed have countless affairs?' It is the contrast between the lover and the bully, or the devoted and the serial cheater, that causes our inner conflict. None of it makes sense. All of it feels confusing. It is through understanding this apparent transformation we bring harmony to our belief and the reality. This is how we restore clarity and peace of mind.

Allow yourself
to grieve the
relationship you
wish you had,
so you can
become
unbound by the
hopes of who
they could be.

Chapter eight:

The Potential

The process of idealise, devalue and discard is a hallmark of emotionally abusive relationships. The relationship begins with intense interest, adoration, and romance and transforms into one of disrespect, secrecy, and control. In a family setting, it may be the abusive parent flips between periods of idealising and devaluing you, or more commonly, they idealise one child whilst devaluing another. These relationships often end in drama and manipulation. Where you feel tossed aside, with no closure or consideration.

Idealisation in itself is not abusive. It is the process of idealisation coupled with abusive tendencies which contributes to establishing control and the power imbalance. The abuser's behaviour whilst they are idealising gets us hooked into the relationship, and then their abusive behaviour begins to permeate it. It is the experience of who they are whilst idealising that keeps us believing in the abuser's potential. Not wanting to give up on them or the connection we believe to be real.

We can characterise idealisation as being held in high esteem and viewed in standards of perfection. The abuser will dote on you, claim you are the image of perfection and everything they could ever hope for. They focus only on your achievements and positive attributes and omit any flaws from the make-up of your character. Some abusers cannot accept 'flaws' in their children or their partner, as they view you as an extension of themselves. Therefore, anything deemed less than perfect threatens their ego and sense of self.

This goes as far as refusing to accept medical conditions, with one survivor speaking of how her abusive ex-husband refused to give consent for prescription glasses for their five-year-old daughter. He stated he believed nothing was 'wrong' with his daughter, although medical results had shown visual impairment, and he did not want her wearing glasses. He suggested pretending to their daughter the doctor had resolved her visual impairment and giving her gummy sweets as a placebo to improve her sight. He insisted no daughter of his would wear glasses. As you can see, his primary concern was denying his daughter had a medical need and maintaining what he viewed as an image of perfection in front of others. In other words; no visible 'weaknesses'.

Through the shine of idealisation, the abuser says things like you're 'soulmates', or you were 'sent from God'. These behaviours help the abuser to establish and reinforce the trauma bond and creates a strong attachment to the potential of the relationship. You feel understood. Connected. Loved. They make promises of a beautiful holiday together, your dream home together, a happy life... together. It is the attachment to how incredible the relationship *could be,* if you could just get past the abusive behaviour, that keeps you holding on. It's a feeling that utopia awaits you if you can remain committed enough to get past the trials and tribulations to get there.

Even if it's been years since the abuser has been the person you believe them to be, you remain attached to the possibility of them becoming that person again. This feeling is strengthened by occasionally seeing glimpses of who you believe to be the 'real them' (the person they are when they are idealising you), keeping the hope alive they could revert to being like that always. This is how the attachment is maintained. There seems to be evidence through your experiences with the abuser that a non-abusive version of them exists. It's not just that you wish the relationship could be different, it's that you have experienced moments when the relationship was how you wanted it to be. This makes it that much harder to let go of the potential.

We find clarity in merging the abuser's behaviour into one whole, instead of seeing them as two fractured people. When you view them as two separate versions of the same person, their potential and who they currently are, you stay attached to an unhealthy reality through the prospect of utopia.

Love Bombing

With love bombing, the abuser overwhelms you with the intensity of their feelings and commitment towards you, which they will ultimately withdraw, causing you to attach and put in the effort to regain it. Some abusers do this consciously, with a callous intention to hook you in. Many, however, are swept up in their own love bombing idealisations, and are driven by other underlying desires, such as the ego boost they receive when you respond positively to their efforts or the sense of control they have over how the relationship develops.

We often think of love bombing as the initial stage of a romantic relationship. For example, the abuser constantly texts or calls you, overwhelming you with their attention and not allowing you time to think or feel anything other than the intense connection developing between you. Early love bombing creates a shortcut to a strong attachment, which is amplified if the attention, affection, and admiration meets your unmet needs. If you feel unheard, unseen, or unworthy, to be showered with attention and affection momentarily meets these needs and you attach quickly to the potential of the relationship.

It can, however, occur throughout the relationship, as well as in other types of abusive relationships. Love bombing in the workplace might be excessive flattery of your professional abilities or what feels like unusually fast involvement with bigger projects. This develops into immense pressure to take on additional responsibilities because they 'took a chance on you'. In a family setting, the parent might shower you with gifts when they overstep a boundary, such as reading your diary or telling the whole family your very personal information. In both incidents, they are overwhelming you with love bombing behaviour. There is the extreme admiration of your professional competence or an enormous display of affection through excessive gift giving. Both invalidate your right to feel upset with their unreasonable expectations or boundary violations, whilst providing you with hope they are capable of meeting your needs and having the relationship you want to have.

Attention, Affection, Admiration

The hallmarks of love bombing are attention, affection and admiration. The abuser gives you constant attention and makes grand gestures. They put you on a pedestal and may themselves seem too good to be true.

They seem to know all the right things to say.

The abuser is meeting your psychological needs through their displays of attention, affection, and admiration. Needs such as belonging and feeling heard, worthy, valued, and enough. The need to be acknowledged and loved. Through its intensity, love bombing meets these needs and takes a shortcut to forming an attachment, but it is not sustained. When the abuser stops love bombing, we are strongly attached, but our needs are no longer being met.

Think of it as two paths that lead to your heart: they can take the long straight road, which requires a substantial amount of effort in terms of time, commitment, dedication, consistency and, dare I say, authenticity. Or there's the quick road, which involves the occasional rock climb, but all that's required is a burst of energy over a short amount of time to secure a place in your heart. More than this, the intensity of the quick road comes with greater feelings of instant gratification compared to the long road, which appeals to the abuser if they are driven by a hyperactive reward system and ego boost.

When the abuser withdraws attention, affection, and admiration, you are already attached to the belief in their potential. You have experienced first-hand they can be affectionate and attentive, so you hold on to the possibility of these attributes resurfacing. The reality is, they only exist in short bursts and are manipulative behaviours, rather than how the abuser behaves consistently towards you.

Fast Pace

Love bombing involves a fast pace to commitment. At the start of the relationship, this can include practical commitments, such as moving in together or taking on bigger work projects. They achieve the fast pace through excessive communication, declarations of love and constant praise. The abuser claims you are soulmates or makes early promises about the future. It's easy to get swept up in the feel good and flattery of love bombing because all the positive attention not only meets our psychological needs, which boosts self-esteem, but also triggers the release of our feel-good hormones.

During the relationship, fast-paced love bombing is the use of grand gestures, gifts, or flattery through admiration. This is to avoid accountability for negative behaviour or having to provide a genuine apology. When the abuser recognises their behaviour has caused you to withdraw from them, they use this fast track to re-establish the emotional connection without having to address the issue or be held accountable. It creates a situation where you feel guilty or as though you are holding onto a grudge. This pressures you into accepting the love bombing gestures and letting go of your rightful hurt, even though the abuser has taken no ownership or tried to rectify it.

The fast pace of love bombing gives you no time or space to think independently of their constant barrage of praise and promises. This is intentional. Even if you have reservations, you have little opportunity to gather your thoughts and become consciously aware of how you feel.

Pressure to Reciprocate

There is a pressure to reciprocate the abuser's level of emotional investment and pace through an implied or stated threat of otherwise losing the relationship. It is not getting swept off your feet, no pressure involved. You may have voiced hesitations at the pace of the relationship only to feel guilt from their inflated disappointment, which is a form of emotional manipulation. Or if you were reluctant to say I love you as quickly as the abuser said it, they withdrew their emotional warmth and expressed 'concern' that you were less emotionally invested than them. This builds pressure for you to make an emotional commitment by using guilt and the fear of losing them to manipulate you. We believe the relationship is currently incredible, and the potential is so promising, so when the abuser subtly pressures us to move at their pace, we brush aside feelings of apprehension because we don't want to regret losing what could be our ideal relationship.

Some survivors describe how they felt special to be 'chosen' by the abuser. The abuser builds an air of superiority or being a saviour, so if they deem you worthy of their attention and admiration, you believe you must be special. It feels good to feel special, especially if we have felt unloved or unseen in our past relationships. We therefore attach quickly and feel pressure to reciprocate to sustain their attention. More than this, however, it is an early set up of the power imbalance. You already go into the relationship feeling as though the abuser is superior and you should feel grateful for their positive attention. You may already feel on edge, *indebted to them*, or unable to understand why they would choose to be with you, causing you to 'put in the work' to maintain their affection.

Extension of Self

Rather than separate identities, abusers see you as an extension of themselves. In this sense, they view your idealised attributes and qualities as a part of them. They also project their own qualities onto you, idealising you through seeing the parts of themselves they admire, *in you*. Beyond this, they view any personal successes or achievements as because of them. They expect you to think, feel, and behave exactly how they would in a situation because they have merged identities. When an abuser says, 'I know what's best for you', it's because they consider it best for themselves and either cannot, or do not want to, consider you as having a separate perspective or needs.

The abuser is projecting their perceived qualities onto you whilst internalising all your qualities as their own, to merge these positive attributes into one identity. They deny you the right to hold a separate space for yourself. This has detrimental effects on wellbeing and self-esteem, as a clear sense of self cannot develop, and you cannot build confidence in your positive attributes and achievements. Instead of believing these qualities or achievements originate in you (they do!), the abuser leads you to believe whatever qualities you possess, they possess to a greater extent. Or any achievements you have made are because of them and they have achieved greater. They undermine your separate sense of self, which can hinder the development of feeling whole or complete without them.

False Self

The false self is an inauthentic or incomplete representation of who the abuser is. They either enrich details of their lives and their character, reflect your own values and what you would be attracted to, or cover up significant parts of themselves that might prevent you from forming an attachment. The abuser may not do this consciously, as if they hold an unstable sense of self or struggle to accept their own flaws and vulnerabilities, they present an idealised version of who they would like to be. *Or of who they try to convince themselves they are.*

The beliefs about the potential of the relationship are based upon the false self. We become attached to this, rather than the reality of the abuser and the relationship.

Embellishments

Abusers exaggerate or lie about their own accomplishments, status, qualities or past to manipulate your perception of them through creating a false image. One survivor said how, on their first date, the abuser told her he could speak French and his family-owned farmland in Africa. She found out over the next 18 months that neither was true. She felt the abuser was obsessed with appearing cultured, when in truth, he had experienced little of other cultures than his own. These fabrications may seem random or irrelevant, but when they are two pieces of a larger puzzle, they contribute to building an entirely different image of the abuser than the reality of who they are. It is the false self we form an attachment to, not the reality.

In other words, the person you formed an attachment to doesn't exist.

Mirroring

Mirroring is something we do to build a connection. We unconsciously imitate other's gestures, body language, words, or speech patterns to build rapport, as we establish connection more easily when there is a shared likeness. Others will do the same to build a connection with us. The abuser, however, mirrors to the extent of imitating your likes and dislikes, your qualities, values and morals or even experiences. This fosters a sense you connect on a deeper level, and they understand you in a way that others cannot.

The abuser lacks a stable sense of self, and therefore copy aspects of your identity to mould their own. One research study associated higher levels of narcissistic traits with higher levels of identity instability, which lead to lower levels of emotional empathy. This explains why some abusers find it difficult to make an emotional connection and could, in part, explain why they seek connection through exaggerated mirroring behaviours. Not only do they have a tendency towards self-serving and lack empathy for others, but they also struggle to make genuine emotional connections through a lack of self-identity. Therefore, they build rapport through copying your interests and agreeing with everything you say. They pay close attention to your qualities, values and morals, because these are likely to be what you find desirable in others, and act accordingly. The issue is this connection is manipulative rather than authentic.

As a result, the qualities you see in the abuser, such as kindness or attentiveness, are actually a reflection of your own qualities.

This encourages the development of a close connection because these qualities will resonate with you, even if you don't consciously recognise them within yourself. Appearing to have so much in common intensifies the attachment and the potential you see in the relationship.

The disconnect with the abuser, however, is they are manipulating your perception of who they are, by covering up parts of themselves through mirroring parts of you. This creates rapport and attachment with a false self, rather than who the abuser genuinely is.

A Double Life

Some abusers present a false self to the extent they lead a double life. One survivor spoke of how she discovered her devoted husband of 25 years had been in a 10-year relationship with another woman. She described how she had to rewrite their history together, including their family holidays, relationship milestones, and her understanding of them as a family unit. She needed to process he had been in a committed relationship with another woman for almost half of their marriage. Another survivor spoke of how when she was due to give birth to her second child, she came to realise her long-term partner had told his work colleagues he was single. Although he had worked there for over six years, and lived with his pregnant partner and older child, he continued to tell them he was a 'bachelor'. She only discovered this truth when he came home and blamed her for the embarrassment of having to 'come clean' to his boss. That he not only had a family, but imminently needed to attend the birth of his second child. She spoke of how deeply wounding it felt that he had simply erased her from existence.

The double life uses a false self to hide significant parts of their character. The abuser may be an active member of the church, involved in the local school or youth club, work for a local charity or volunteer at the nearby animal shelter. They will help members of the wider family, friends, acquaintances and community with enthusiasm and pleasure. Or perhaps they are adventurous, with big plans to travel and see the world, appearing open, warm and engaged. This is the person you meet. This is the person you form an attachment to. However, when you enter the reality of living with them, they are polar opposite. The false self they present is a major cover up for their abusive tendencies in the home.

This extends to hiding significant details of their life. The abuser appears devoted to you and your children, only for you to discover they were having multiple affairs or even living with a secret family elsewhere. Or they have built an entire identity based upon being a successful, wealthy, businessperson who frequently goes on work trips, only to discover they are penniless with no work ethic and involved in fraudulent activities. Again, you form an attachment to the false self. When you discover the reality, the shock is distressing, as it fractures your understanding of your world in a moment.

It's challenging to come to terms with the abuser's double life because it is a huge betrayal. It is also the enormity of dissonance between who you believe them to be and the reality. There is a process of revisiting your memories and reforming them, to incorporate your new understanding of what was happening in the relationship, such as if they were having a long-term or multiple affairs. If you have experienced this, know it was not your fault. You are not naïve. It was information that was deliberately kept from you.

You are not to blame for being trusting, loyal and loving. These are beautiful qualities.

Future Faking

Future faking creates a strong attachment to the abuser through promises of the amazing future you can have together. These promises are based on your hopes and life goals, which means you are already emotionally attached to the outcome. This keeps you invested in the relationship's potential, even though the abuser makes no authentic effort to follow through. You don't want to give up on them. In addition, you don't want to give up on the opportunity of fulfilling your life aspirations, *with them*.

Empty Promises

If you wish you could spend more time with your children or have a beautiful family home, the abuser will promise to make this happen. If you hope to travel and see the world, the abuser will vow to travel with you. You long for a deep, committed relationship, and the abuser reiterates how they feel the same and promises eternal commitment. Or, as a child, you relied on them for facilitating your interests and growth, and they always promised investing in you 'tomorrow'. *But it always comes with a catch*. Whilst they ask you to make sacrifices for the good of the relationship or expect you to be grateful for how much they have provided so far, the promises don't get closer to materialising.

Future faking is a manipulation tool. The abuser listens to your hopes and lures you in with enticing promises. These promises are another way to control how the relationship develops. They lure you into making major decisions and commitments quickly, which the abuser can then take advantage of. These decisions include moving in together, moving away from your support system, or investing your money into the relationship. It may be a decision to forgive the abuser once again or to give them the benefit of the doubt for their unacceptable behaviour. By the time you discover it was an empty promise, the abuser has already established a power imbalance, making it much harder for you to change the course of the relationship or break free.

Some abusers never intended to follow through on these promises. They simply said what they knew would lead to the desired outcome of getting you hooked into the relationship. This feeds into their need for power and control. Others genuinely believe their own promises. Abusers like the image of themselves rather than their authentic self, so fantasising about being the person who fulfils your dreams gives them an inflated sense of self-worth and importance. The issue is, once they devalue you, they have little commitment to follow through on their spoken promises. The image no longer provides them with a sense of fulfilment. *It is no longer serving them.* They say, 'I never said that', and 'you really believed that would happen?', or accuse you of not fulfilling their expectations, hence they lay the blame for the broken promises at your feet.

Ultimately, you discover the reality of living with the abuser is not the same as what they promised. Yet, even long after the relationship ends, we still feel attached to the empty promises of the future, harbouring feelings of sadness and regret.

Actions versus Words

Future faking works by keeping you invested in the hope of the future, so you tolerate the abusive behaviour of the present.

The potential of your future with the abuser acts as an invisibility cloak for the reality of the relationship, and this cloak is made of their convincing words. They say what you want to hear but take no action to follow through. They say they will drink less, save more, or treat you with respect, but continue to drink more, spend more, and treat you with disdain.

You don't process the abusive behaviour, however, because through their words, your attention is directed towards the abuser's potential. You may not even recognise it is abuse because of the discord that develops between how they are behaving and what they are saying the future could hold. Their words provide hope, which is soothing when you are experiencing the hurt of abusive behaviour, so you continue to look towards the brighter future together as a coping mechanism. It feels too painful to give up on the hope.

This is where we should pay attention to behaviour because actions speak louder than words, but my goodness, the future faking words can be deafening.

Red Flags

Red flags are behaviours that give you reason to stop and take time to seriously reflect on the direction of the relationship. Many red flags are subtle in the early stages. They leave you with a feeling something isn't quite right. We intuitively sense this, yet a problem is we have learned to doubt our intuition. Or perhaps to disconnect from it completely. It's challenging to know what your intuition is, what is being triggered or whether you simply feel numb, and this makes it hard to identify red flags.

Red flags themselves offer comfort when they are familiar, because familiarity feels safe, even if it isn't the case. This means if you have experienced unhealthy relationships, entering a healthy relationship may feel less safe than one where there are red flags. We know how to navigate red flag behaviour, whereas healthier relationships can feel uncomfortable, triggering, and have us running in the other direction.

Clarity is key.

This will help you recognise unhealthy behaviour and learn to reconnect to your intuition. Even when idealising, the abuser has a drive for control, so there are signs the relationship is heading towards an abusive dynamic. If the relationship is already established, there are behaviours and attitudes that can help you identify a pattern of abuse.

Second, reflect on how the behaviour affects you and the relationship. For example, we can all be jealous sometimes. It doesn't mean we are all abusive. It is their actions and impact of jealousy which can help you identify it as a red flag. Such as, do they limit access to your phone or make wild accusations which you have to defend yourself against? Do you feel heightened anxiety due to their jealous outbursts and feel they restrict your freedom because of it?

Even if the behaviour doesn't signal abuse, if it doesn't sit right with you, it warrants your pause and reflection. Ask yourself, how do I feel about this? Do I like the direction this is heading? Am I making excuses for their behaviour? Can I communicate with them about it? *Is this what I want in my relationship?*

Short Cuts

- Moving fast
- Saying you're perfect
- High intensity
- Jealousy
- Controlling behaviour

High emotional intensity, pressuring you to commit quickly in the relationship, bombarding you with communication or insisting you spend all your time together, are signs of manipulating you into a quick attachment. Seeing you as perfect, their soulmate or sent from God, are signs of idealising behaviour rather than an authentic connection. The rush of intense emotions is a product of infatuation, lust or the ideals they have assigned to you and the relationship. This is a red flag of love bombing.

Controlling behaviour and excessive jealousy indicate someone may have possessive tendencies. Coupled with the love bombing, these shortcuts to attachment signal they feel they have a right to control you and the relationship.

Reflection

Take a moment to pause and ask yourself, 'how am I feeling'? Bring awareness to your gut feeling about the pace of the relationship. Do you feel pressured to reciprocate the level of emotional investment and match the speed at which the relationship is progressing? Or is there mutual agreement over the development of the relationship? In a healthy relationship, you should be able to voice your concerns and preferences, to try and find a way to move forward that satisfies you both.

Disrespect

- Disrespectful towards friends or family
- 'Crazy exes'
- Guilts you
- Cruel or criticising
- Subtle aggression

Disrespectful behaviour might not be aimed towards you. It could be they are disrespectful towards your friends, other road users, or to restaurant staff. Or all their exes are labelled crazy. They make cruel comments disguised as jokes, or frequently criticise others. They show subtle aggression towards people who disagree with them. These are red flags of entitlement and a lack of tolerance for others. Even if this behaviour is not directed towards you, it is a warning sign, if you fall out of favour, this will be how they treat you.

It is also a sign for potential isolation, as it builds an 'us against them' mentality, where you feel pressured to withdraw from others. The abuser holds an attitude that no one else is worthy of your time. They may begin to think negatively of you if you continue to spend time with others. They imply you are 'just the same as everybody else' if you continue to want to socialise. This brings instability into the relationship and pressures you to choose between the potential of the relationship or socialising with your friends.

Reflection

Observing their disrespectful behaviour towards others shows you they lack tolerance for opinions or perspectives other than their own, and therefore indirectly teaches you to censor yourself in the relationship. Ask yourself whether you feel free to express your opinion or a differing perspective, or whether you feel on edge, nervous or unsure about how they will react. Do you feel as though they expect a certain perspective or opinion from you? Or are you criticised, put down, or your perspective is invalidated? Possibly disguised as jokes.

Inconsistency

- Double standards
- Mood flips easily
- Behaviour and words don't match
- Disguised admissions
- Unwillingness to compromise

Inconsistent behaviour can signify a lack of authenticity and an attitude of entitlement. If the abuser is attempting to manipulate you into becoming emotionally attached, there may be certain behaviours that don't match who they claim to be. These include sudden aggressive outbursts or blowing hot and cold, even though they swear they are committed. Some abusers make disguised admissions early on, such as saying, 'I hope I don't break your heart'. Or they constantly speak of their trustworthiness and how they will treat you well, as if they need to convince you they will not descend into their abusive tendencies in the future.

An unwillingness to compromise and double standards also show a sense of entitlement, where they consider their needs greater than those of others. They hold you to certain expectations but do not hold themselves to the same standards, such as always expecting you to respond to texts or be punctual, whereas they always run late and respond to your texts intermittently. This may be a warning sign for controlling behaviour and a dismissive attitude towards your mutual needs, hinting towards the power imbalance that develops in abusive relationships.

Reflection

Do you feel they say all the right things, but the relationship is one sided in terms of how much you give and who compromises? Do you have an uneasy feeling, but you can't put your finger on it? Does their behaviour feel inconsistent; do they blow hot and cold, or does their charm seem to switch on and off? Explore where the uneasy feeling is coming from. Is it your intuition telling you something? Is the relationship heading in a direction you are happy with? Are you able to communicate with them about your need for greater consistency?

5 relationship green flags:

- o **Open Communication:** listens, compromises, uses a calm and rational tone, can apologise, freedom to express yourself, and can have hard conversations.
- o **Trust:** honesty, consistent behaviour, being accountable, and an ability to cope with outside challenges.
- o **Respect:** shows genuine concern, empathy, partnership, not ownership, and equality in the relationship.
- o **Supports Growth:** supports ambitions, celebrates your achievements with you, shows care and encouragement in difficult times.
- o **Honouring Separate Identities (as well as forming a shared relationship identity):** honouring boundaries, interest in one another's values, respecting your differences, and an effort to understand and respect you as an individual.

Chapter nine:

The Reality

Where the idealising behaviour attaches you to the potential of the relationship, it is through the devaluing behaviours we feel the conflict of dissonance.

Idealisation and devaluing are part of the splitting concept, whereby a person views others as either 'all good' or 'all bad'. When you are being idealised, your positive attributes are exaggerated; when you are being devalued, they view you through a negative lens. These processes are not only present in abusive relationships. They are also a part of normal childhood development, such as young children having idealised views of their parents, or adolescence having idealised views of their friends when they are carving a separate identity from their family. We also engage in splitting as adults when we go through a stressful time, to help us compartmentalise and therefore manage and process feelings of anxiety. When it is part of an abusive dynamic, however, the abuser is in a chronic state of idealising and devaluing as how they view the world, and these attitudes can lead to abusive behaviours towards others.

As the relationship with the abuser develops, and you cannot live up to the idealised image, they become resentful towards you. Any negative emotions could trigger the devaluing process, such as feeling challenged, threatened, or disappointed. It isn't only conflict that can trigger these emotions. It can be any range of healthy interactions, such as differing opinions or a misinterpreted facial expression, which is why, even before the devaluing begins, you may feel unease. You unconsciously sense the lack of constancy in the abuser and, therefore, lack of security in the relationship. When faced with these negative emotions, the splitting of you into either 'all good' or 'all bad' provides the abuser with justification to be abusive. They criticise you, put you down, belittle you and show their disappointment, directing their negative energy towards you.

The stark contrast between being placed on a pedestal to being treated like the dirt under their shoe is a tough emotional journey. It is in part the immensity in the contrast of their behaviour which makes it so unbelievable. It doesn't seem to make sense they would become so disdainful for no obvious reason. We therefore conclude something must have happened in the relationship that caused their behaviour to change. It seems to be the only logical explanation. What this conclusion leads you to believe, however, is it's in your power to change it back. Here begin the attempts to please and appease the abuser and restore the relationship. In reality, nothing happened in the relationship. The shift is because of the abuser's inner world; their discomfort and need for control.

It is through devaluing behaviours we experience covert abuse. The psychological games, highly critical and neglectful attitudes, relationship instability and control. The relationship covertly transitions from idealising to devaluing, and many survivors find this process happens without their recognition. This creates further confusion, of finding ourselves in the grasp of an abusive relationship, when everything had seemed so idyllic.

Abuse is Gradual

You may be familiar with the fable of the boiling frog.

If you put a frog into boiling water, it will detect the danger and immediately jump out to safety. If you put a frog into tepid water, however, and slowly bring it to the boil, the frog won't notice the danger and therefore remains in the water and cooks to death. It cannot detect the gradual increase in temperature until it's too late.

The premise of the story is we accept subtle and steady changes, even if these are building towards negative consequences. This explains the acceptance of the devaluing process and abuse. The increase in abuse is gradual. We would never tolerate the level of abuse that develops in the relationship if it started at that level, nor would we if there was an abrupt curtain drop and overnight, all interactions became abusive. Like a gradual increase of alcohol or spicy foods raises our tolerance level, it is the subtle and steady transition in the relationship that increases our tolerance for unacceptable behaviour. The truth of experiencing abuse goes undetected, until we are immersed by it.

The gradual nature of increasing abuse makes the reality of the relationship difficult to identify, which keeps you believing in its potential.

A Question of Character

The transition between behaviours that arise from idealising and devaluing is subtle and can be difficult to process. We form a strong attachment to the 'idealiser', and therefore, the devaluing behaviour seems completely out of character. When they show abusive behaviour, we draw conclusions. We think they must have had a hard day, rather than recognising their tendency towards abuse. Worse still, is when you conclude you must have overstepped the line for them to behave that way. This leads you to censor your behaviour. You don't want to be 'insensitive', and the feeling of walking on eggshells begins. The gradual shift in their behaviour makes it difficult to recognise the abusive behaviour is very much a part of their character and not just a one off.

Boundary Pushing

Another way abuse creeps into the relationship is through a subtle overstepping of boundaries. The abuser pushes on your boundaries using manipulative tactics, such as guilt or gaslighting, fostering doubt as to whether your boundaries are acceptable. Each time you move a boundary, they will push for it to be moved further in their favour. For example, they always run thirty minutes late when you meet with friends, and they gradually increase this to an hour and then longer still until you have to cancel on your plans. When you raise the issue with them, they feign offense and claim you're selfish. They remind you how they do everything they can to be home in time, and how ungrateful you are. They imply the 'person they love' would never act so selfishly, with an unspoken threat of rejection (or punishment) if you raise the issue again. This leaves you questioning your boundary, choosing next time, to just cancel your plans.

Here, the abuser has isolated you using covert abuse. They have deflected and shifted blame and shamed you for having needs and wanting to socialise. They pushed on boundaries by using guilt, so you feel unreasonable for asking them to honour their commitments. Boundary pushing contributes towards the power imbalance, where we begin to walk on eggshells and question our own behaviour, as the abuser's needs become central in the relationship.

Reasonable Reasons

During the relationship, the abuser presents reasonable reasons for their behaviour. These are excuses which undermine the validity of your reaction. The abuser will present a reason which causes you to doubt whether it's fair for you to be upset by their behaviour or hold them accountable. When they do this frequently, it leads you to question whether it's in fact your responses that are unreasonable. You lose trust in your ability to perceive the situation correctly, as well as confidence in your own behaviour. You may question how you are treating them, or believe you think the worst of them. This leads us to believe we need to work harder or 'be better', to stop being judgemental or expecting 'too much'. We try to censor our reaction to their abuse, believing there is a reasonable reason for it, whereas our response is unreasonable.

Once again, they shift your attention from the unreasonable behaviour onto your reasonable response. More than this, as the relationship develops, you may make up 'reasonable reasons' for their behaviour yourself, as your trust in your own perception dwindles and you become more reliant on their version of reality.

Unable to Identify

Our beliefs about abusive relationships, and what society tells us about them, may not match what it feels like to experience abuse. This makes it difficult to identify the relationship as abusive when there are subtle shifts in their behaviour. It is hard to find the words to describe what is happening, because although you are experiencing abuse, it doesn't look and feel like how you expect abuse to be. This leaves you feeling confused and unable to recognise the reality of the relationship. The abuse therefore goes undetected until you are much deeper into the relationship, or often, survivors only have this realisation after the relationship has ended and they begin to process in full the abusive experiences.

Commitment Crux

Many survivors find, with every commitment made, the level of abuse increases. This is what I name the commitment crux. For example, when you are first dating, everything seems ideal. You decide to move in together, and this is when the abuser starts their demeaning behaviour towards you. It seems completely out of character, so you don't read it as a warning sign. You put it down to a phase or give them the benefit of the doubt. When you move to a new neighbourhood, however, the verbal abuse begins. It is now harder for you to hold them accountable or consider leaving, because of the practical difficulties that come with having just relocated. You are also more emotionally invested, and therefore, more dependent on the hope it could return to happier times. You begin to question whether it's your perception that's off. Maybe they are only verbally aggressive because you are immature, needy, or selfish, like they keep saying you are. If you stopped messing up, everything could go back to normal. That's what they tell you. That's what you start to tell yourself.

You see glimmers of the 'old them', giving you hope things could return to how they were. So, you get engaged, and with engagement comes physical intimidation. Now, you feel you are in too deep. Everyone thinks you have the perfect relationship. You've made a lot of commitments, and this relationship is now a major part of your life and who you are. It's a lot harder to walk away from.

And that's if you even have clarity to think so clearly.

Often, by this point, there is heavy confusion, and we cannot see whether their behaviour is unreasonable or whether we are causing them to behave in such a volatile way because we are the problem.

They would have you believe this.

The abuse continues to escalate the more you commit to the relationship. This is because of the emotional and practical ties. The stronger these ties are, the harder it is for you to cut them, even when facing abusive behaviour. You feel trapped, and in this sense, believing in the relationship's potential is a coping mechanism to counter the feeling of helplessness.

Acknowledging the reality when you feel unable to do anything about it can be overwhelming, so holding onto the potential is a way to ease the stress. It offers hope when you feel trapped in an unhealthy environment.

Emotional & Practical Commitments

Practical commitments include moving in together, moving area, engagement, marriage, or children. It can also include dependency, such as if the abuser controls access to money, if you depend on them for your medical needs, if they are your parent or if they are your boss. There may even be role reversal, where the abuser expects you to financially provide or care for them. You become committed to the relationship by feeling responsible for them, which can feel just as trapping.

Emotional commitment includes putting your trust in them, putting your hope into the relationship, allowing yourself to believe they are authentic, or having a strong desire for the relationship to work out. As you become more dependent on the relationship, such as if you move out of area and lose social connections, you also become more emotionally dependent on the abuser. This facilitates stronger emotional commitment as you look to them to fulfil your emotional needs.

The more emotionally invested you are, the more difficult it is to walk away. The more practical ties you have, the more difficult it becomes literally to leave, even with the increase in abusive behaviour. As a result, you tolerate a higher level of abuse than you would have prior to the relationship commitments. When someone says, 'I would never let someone treat me that way', they lack awareness of this process.

There is no shame for how long you stayed in the relationship or the level of abuse you endured. The combination of the gradual increase of abuse and becoming trapped through commitments means the water is boiling before you realise. And by this point, there are limited options to get out of the boiling pot.

5 reflective questions to explore in the relationship:

- o Do their actions match their words?
- o Do I often make excuses for their behaviour?
- o Is there a pattern of disregarding my boundaries and my separate needs or commitments (such as work or social commitments)?
- o Do I feel conflicted about them, such as I feel they are loving towards me, but I also feel nervous around them, or feel their behaviour and affection is inconsistent or unpredictable?
- o Do I feel unsettled, unhappy, or uneasy, but feel unable to identify why?

Chapter ten:

Reconciling Dissonance

Following on from being idealised and devalued, you may experience the discard, which is essentially abandonment. We commonly think of the discard as the end of the relationship. However, episodes of abandonment can happen within the relationship, which don't involve the formal 'break up-make up'. This is true of abusive family members too. Here, abandonment involves the abuser blocking all communication and positive connection, whilst smearing your name to friends or family members. This can last indefinitely, only for them to start talking to you again as if they only spoke to you yesterday. Their abandonment simply erased from existence. It is not, however, erased from your memory.

Cognitive dissonance between the belief in the abuser's potential and the reality of the relationship is a major cause of inner conflict, which can long outlast the end of the relationship. More than this, the abuser seeks to maintain your belief in their potential, even after they have abandoned you, as they are still driven by the need for power and control. This can take on different forms. They may intermittently show up to idealise you, or indirectly maintain your belief in their potential through the picture-perfect image of their new relationship. Or they become vengeful, where they are aggressive and abusive towards you, but show the potential of how kindly they could treat you through how they behave towards others.

It is through integrating your understanding of who they are with your experiences that you reconcile dissonance. This will reduce inner conflict and weaken the attachment to their potential. It enables you to reflect on your experiences with greater clarity and to empower yourself to make conscious and clear decisions about how to manage your relationship with the abuser.

Shifting focus onto your growth.

Abandonment Fears

Abandonment fears affect the behaviour, choices and responses of both the abuser and survivor in different ways. Fear of abandonment is a contributing factor to the abuser's controlling behaviour, and the survivor's vulnerability.

For the Abuser

In the book, Group Work with Populations at Risk, Steven Stosny discusses how a key contributor to an abuser's behaviour and unwillingness to change is a deficit in affect regulation. This is an ability to manage and appropriately respond to their emotions. It leads to an inability to process guilt, shame, and abandonment fears effectively. Instead, they convert these vulnerable feelings to anger which lead to the patterns of abusive control in the home.

Fear of abandonment and a need for control contribute to the abuser abandoning others. Essentially, they abandon you so you cannot abandon them. The intense closeness and positive feelings associated with idealising you are replaced with feelings of shame, anger and resentment during the devaluing process, and the abuser blames these feelings on you. They feel disempowered because of this and try to maintain control by attacking your self-esteem.

On the one hand, they believe you will never leave them because they tell themselves you can't do better than them. Your self-esteem is low, and they have manipulated the situation successfully so far. On the other hand, they hold a deep fear of being abandoned. They may even view your attempts to hold them accountable or your 'negative' reaction to their abuse as abandonment within the relationship, as you no longer view them as perfect. This threatens their ego and triggers their fear you will leave them. So, they maintain control by abandoning you first.

The abuser dresses this up, however, to make it seem far more glamourous. They appear to be having the time of their life, or to have found a partner they deeply love after years of you experiencing indifference. *They appear to be fulfilling their potential.* This strengthens the belief things could have been different between you and the fear you were the problem all along. Really, it's just smoke and mirrors. They are covering up the fear of abandonment, need to control and the beginning of idealisation directed elsewhere. When you get to know the parts of them they don't want to see, they run away to situations or people who don't know any better, so they don't have to face them. This is so positive feelings can once again override feelings of shame, guilt and abandonment fears, which they struggle to process.

Alternatively, the relationship becomes a self-fulfilling prophecy. Through their emotionally and psychologically abusive behaviour, the abuser behaves in ways that are unacceptable and eventually forces you to end the relationship. The abuser avoids vulnerability by sabotaging the relationship from the start. Then, they can claim they were right never to trust you. You abandoned them. Just like 'they knew you would'. This is a form of maintaining control. It can lead to survivors struggling with guilt as, if the abuser has a history of being abandoned, the survivor feels they are another person who has let them down. You may also feel it is because of your own 'shortcomings' – not being kind, patient or supportive enough – that the abuser could not fulfil their potential.

It is important to recognise the abuser is engaging in behaviour and choices that lead to a repetition of harmful cycles and feelings of abandonment. They created an environment that was unsafe for you. They are creating a self-fulfilling prophecy. You didn't abandon them for choosing to leave an abusive relationship. And it is not your responsibility to make them stay. They are responsible for their behaviour and regardless of the reasons they abuse, there is no justification for it. You should not feel guilty for prioritising your safety. No matter if they are struggling or hurt, abuse is still a choice.

For the Survivor

For survivors, there's a risk the abuser will take advantage of our vulnerability. When we have abandonment wounds, we are more likely to over share or over explain ourselves, for fear of being judged harshly, misunderstood and then abandoned. We may have learned from a young age love was not provided consistently and was based upon performing and proving we were good enough. This leads to over explaining and over sharing to defend our worth and avoid being abandoned.

In an abusive dynamic, the abuser uses this vulnerable information to gain further control. They threaten to share private details or use it to draw others into conflict with you, creating more tension in your environment and less support in your relationships. Or, they learn your deeper vulnerabilities, such as a fear of becoming like your mother, and use this as ammunition during confrontations, firing, 'you're just like your mother', to manipulate and wound you and draw you into submission.

A fear of abandonment also contributes towards the pain experienced when the abuser discards us, as this experience is akin to one of our core fears (being abandoned) becoming a reality. According to Maslow's hierarchy of needs, our basic psychological needs include the need to feel safe, the need to feel loved and belong, and the need to develop our self-esteem. The discard falls short of these needs. The discard, which is abandonment rather than a healthy separation, does not allow for you to integrate the loss of the relationship with minimal psychological harm. Instead of maintaining a level of safety, belonging, and self-esteem during the separation, the experience of abandonment intensifies the pain.

The issue with abandonment is, it does not provide you with any closure and it is emotionally wounding. This leaves you vulnerable to being drawn back to the abuser if they begin idealising you once again. The affection, attention and admiration soothe the intense emotional pain of having been abandoned. If it is indeed the final discard, then the lack of closure makes it difficult to process the reality of your experiences and, therefore, the belief of what could have been remains prominent in your mind.

This is not to feel shame. This is to remove shame; to understand the continued attachment and dismantle the belief. When we experience psychological harm, we search to create psychological safety in other ways. The reason we hold on to our belief in the abuser is because of the impact of abuse: the manipulation, the trauma bonding and the confusion, and because they denied us closure. The belief reduces the pain of the experience. It plays a role in your survival. Over time, however, it becomes a sticking point in your growth that creates further conflict and confusion. When you feel like this, consider it may be time to say to yourself:

'Thank you to myself for protecting me with this belief. To honour my continued growth, it is now time for me to let it go.'

Abrupt Emotional Disconnection

What I understand is, regardless of the circumstances, a common source of pain for survivors is the abrupt emotional disconnection. The circumstances under which this happens create their own unique pain points, yet the hurt caused by the abruptness of the disconnection is the same.

There are survivor stories of infidelity, double lives, forced abortions and paternity tests or just walking out the door and never coming back. The common source of pain across these circumstances, however, is the suddenness with which the abuser switches off their feelings. It is as though in a breath they went from a strong emotional connection to feeling nothing. Even if you ended the relationship, this is true. The abuser seems to hijack your choice and cut you off emotionally. There may be a short intense burst of declaring love or attempts to keep you attached, but if these fail, they suddenly withdraw.

In contrast to many experiences, one survivor explained how when her relationship ended, her abuser was extremely amicable, wished her well, and then she never heard from him again. Although it seems like a blessing, it caused a huge amount of pain, confusion, self-doubt and lingering inner conflict about the abuse she endured during the relationship. And it still ended with an abruptness of disconnection and lack of closure. The contrast in behaviour during the relationship and separation, coupled with the fact it is outside of 'the norm' for abusive relationship endings, caused a significant rupture in clarity of her experiences. This delayed her gaining closure and shifting focus away from the abusive relationship and onto personal growth.

Here, we can see how it does not differ from other abusive relationship endings. By denying closure, the abuser keeps you confused and in a state of self-doubt, therefore focused on the relationship and what could have been, rather than able to move on and begin to thrive without them. This enables the abuser to maintain a sense of power and control over you and the end of the relationship.

One explanation for the abrupt emotional disconnection is attachment deficits in the abuser. Attachment deficits are the inability to form sustainable attachments, and there is overwhelming evidence abusers have issues with this. Regardless of gender or sexual orientation, abusers in intimate relationships have difficulties with intimacy, mutuality, trust, compassion, jealousy, fear of abandonment and fear of loss of self. These difficulties affect their ability to form viable connections with others, which is why they seem to sever their feelings for you abruptly.

The difficulties come when we internalise the abrupt disconnection. At a time when you are still processing the relationship, coming to terms with its ending, and trying to gain closure you then believe their ability to disconnect abruptly is a reflection on you. On how loveable and worthy you are. The important message is the abrupt disconnection is not because of you or a reflection of your worth. It is the abuser's inability to sustain attachment with others.

Stoking the Belief

Abusers commonly have low self-esteem, or fragile high self-esteem. Both result in the abuser seeking validation through the attention and praise of others, and a preoccupation with how others perceive them. As they don't have a stable sense of self, their worth is gained through their image. Therefore, they will go to great lengths to protect it. Further to this, abusers with fragile high self-esteem, such as being highly narcissistic, have a sense of superiority which manifests through displays of dominance or entitlement. This is why the end of the relationship is a particularly dangerous time for survivors, where the abuser experiences a 'collapse' of esteem because of the heightened threat to their image, along with the threat of the loss of control, and respond with extreme hostility or defensiveness.

The threat comprises a loss of control over the perception you and others have of them and losing the validation you give them. The abuser seeks to minimise the threat to their esteem by maintaining your belief in their potential and their constructed image. This is how they hold on to power. If you maintain the belief in their falsified reality, you remain emotionally connected, even if you are no longer physically in a relationship with them. This minimises the risk of you holding them accountable for the abuse and injuring their esteem, and allows them to hold on to your attention, giving them continued validation. It also reduces the threat of others realizing their abusive behaviour, as the belief creates conflict and uncertainty in your truth.

In other words, damage control and sustaining validation, otherwise referred to as 'supply'. The abuser doesn't want their carefully constructed image threatened by you breaking free of them and telling your truth. They don't want you to recognise who they truly are, they don't want others to see this, and they don't want to be confronted with it themselves.

This is a further reason it continues to prove difficult to recognise the reality of your experiences. The abuser actively attempts to maintain your belief in the distorted reality and in their potential. It is a continuation of the abusive mindset – targeting your thoughts and feelings to maintain control - that extends beyond the end of the relationship.

Hoovering

- Promises to change
- Apparent accountability

- Highlighting their role (you or the children NEED them)
- Placing blame for the 'broken' relationship on to you
- Declarations of love
- Refusing to acknowledge the relationship is over

As the name suggests, hoovering is the abuser's attempt to suck you back into the vortex of the relationship. There are two key components of attempts to hoover: they feel like they can succeed, and it suits them to try.

First, think about an actual vacuum cleaner. When you vacuum in your living room, you don't try to suck up anything in the hallway. You know you haven't got a chance. You focus on sucking in what's possible. The same goes for the abuser. They are only going to try to hoover you in if they believe you are still emotionally within reach. Like with other emotionally and psychologically abusive behaviours, they use your emotions and your thoughts against you to draw you back in. If they do not feel like they can succeed, they won't even try for fear of looking foolish, for fear of rejection, and for fear of giving you power.

Second, it must suit them to try. If they are idealising someone else, they are unlikely to turn their attention to hoovering you. They may, however, engage in these behaviours six months or two years down the line when they suddenly reappear in your life. They stoke the connection to gain a sense of power and validation by re-establishing the abusive dynamic.

Hoovering behaviour is momentary changes in behaviour or words that create a surge of doubt about giving up on your belief in the relationship. The aim is to have you overrun by doubt, so you fear you are making a terrible mistake. The fear of ending the relationship must be smaller than the fear of staying in the relationship, and hoovering relies on these doubts and fears to keep you attached.

Abusers introduce the possibility of change through promises, declarations of love and affection, apologies, or apparent accountability. If it's the first time they've expressed a desire to change or acknowledged their abusive behaviour, it is very tempting to see it as a turning point. The reality is their words are rarely backed up by actions. It is like an inverted form of gaslighting; instead of denying, they are acknowledging, instead of shifting blame, they are saying they need to change. Yet, it is still manipulation. They rely on your hope things could be different between you, and once you invest fully into the relationship again, they return to denying and blame-shifting their behaviour.

Abusers also stick to the formula of using guilt, fear and pressure during hoovering. One survivor shared how when she was leaving her abusive husband, he told her if their five-year-old grew up to commit suicide because she was bullied for coming from a broken home, their child's blood was on her hands. No parent would be unaffected by these words. Other forms of guilt or pressure come through bombarding you with contact, stalking (either physically or on social media) or refusing to accept the end of the relationship. These are displays of dominance. The abuser gives you the impression life won't be better without them, so staying is your best choice.

Victimhood

Abusers view themselves as a victim of circumstances. They either believe we have not given them the special treatment they deserve, or we have forced them into their abusive behaviour. Either way, they are not taking accountability for their actions, preferring to view themselves as a victim of the inaccurate perceptions of others.

If the abuser feels superior, they believe they are entitled to behave how they see fit, not how society dictates. They also feel they should be given special treatment, which is however they deem appropriate, even if we consider this controlling. Therefore, they feel constrained by social rules and moral guidelines that prevent them from being able to give as little and receive as much as they want in their relationships. In their mind, they have not been given the special treatment they deserve, and they are the victim of these circumstances.

Alternatively, the abuser will look to blame their behaviour on everything and anything other than themselves. Not only is blame shifted onto you, but also other people, life events, the past, the current situation, or the future. They view themselves as a powerless victim. Chronically misunderstood. Never accountable for their own actions. Never the source of their own abusive behaviour.

The victim mentality of the abuser means at the point of separation, they often view themselves as the victim of the relationship. They believe you either didn't give them what they deserved, or you are to blame for their abusive behaviour and the tensions. They shift responsibility for the breakdown of the relationship onto you and continue to view themselves as the victim of circumstance.

The burden of having full responsibility of the breakdown of the relationship pinned on you is another weight to carry when you are already trying to cope with the effects of abuse. The abuser's unwavering belief you have wronged them increases the confusion and doubt about your own behaviour. It makes it harder to separate the distorted reality of the abuser and the reality of what you've experienced.

Smear Campaign

To create doubt in your truth and discredit your voice, the abuser engages in a smear campaign. It is an attempt to minimise the threat to their sense of self and potential damage to their image, posed by you speaking out about your experiences. The abuser will 'prep' others, so if you decide to tell them about the abuse, are receiving this information through a filtered lens; a lens that paints you in an unfavourable light and evokes empathy for the abuser.

Again, this reinforces the abusive narratives of the relationship. That it is your reaction that's the problem, not the abusive behaviour, and it's your perception of the relationship that is wrong. It is also a continuation of isolating you from being able to access support. We lean on those close to us when we go through a major transition. But through the smear campaign, the abuser cuts off your access to effective emotional support, maintaining your dependence on them for an emotional connection. This is a power play by the abuser and increases the chance you will turn back towards the relationship with them.

Additionally, survivors will do things in the relationship that seem counterintuitive to being abused. One survivor gifted her abuser a knife, even though she was physically afraid of him. Or simply, going on holiday, attending a friend's wedding, having children together, all seemingly blissfully happy, appear to contradict the possibility of them being an abuser. This becomes part of the smear campaign, with the abuser claiming, 'but they gifted me a knife, how could they be afraid of me?!', or 'but you remember how happy we were together back then!'.

These experiences, however, do not contradict the presence of abuse. We build our walls to protect ourselves during the relationship, and this includes painting on a smile. You may not have recognised the abuse, you hold onto the good times, and your needs become secondary. You do things to please the abuser, to try and keep them happy and avoid further abuse. *You will have been silenced.* When you leave the relationship, this becomes clearer, and you begin to tell your story.

I'm so sorry, if when you've spoken about abuse, someone's response was to give the abuser the benefit of the doubt and to question your morals for talking about it.

Impairing Self-Sufficiency

Preventing you from becoming self-sufficient and independent from the abuser is an attempt to teach you that life is not better, *or possible*, without them. They want to show you in no uncertain terms that you need them in order to function. The abuser targets core needs: financial security, your business, your home, your connection to family and your children, and your reputation (social belonging). They might make false allegations to police, social services or mental health professionals, or cut off financial support, withhold mortgage payments or target your place of work.

This is a display of dominance. Some abusers even tell you they will set out to destroy you. It is a way of maintaining the belief life is better with the abuser. Even though you are unhappy, life without them appears unviable. Although it is not maintaining the belief in their potential, it is maintaining the belief that staying with the abuser is your best option.

Letting Go of the Belief

It is one thing to recognise the belief and reality of the abuser don't match. It is another thing to bring harmony between how you feel, what you believe, and what you have experienced. You may feel as if the belief in the abuser's potential is your default setting. With this belief as your baseline, it is a continuous effort to keep your feelings, thoughts, and experiences in sync rather than fall back to the confusion and inner conflict of their reality. *And the hope of what could have been.*

Letting go of the belief feels painful because it provided hope when you felt trapped. It feels like giving up on someone you don't want to lose. Believing things could get better helped reduce the pain of the relationship. Therefore, no longer believing in them can feel unsafe and deeply upsetting because it was protecting you from the pain of your experiences.

How good would it feel, though, to replace your belief in their potential with belief in yourself? To trust in how you experienced the relationship, not how they tell you it was?

When you let go of the belief in the abuser's potential you create space to believe in yourself. With belief in yourself, you become less conflicted about what could have been and trust in the reality of your experiences. The new belief becomes your default setting, allowing your thoughts, feelings, and experiences to build harmoniously.

You can let go of the belief through:

Grief

Grieving for the loss of a relationship that was harmful might feel like your emotions are betraying you. Are you even allowed to grieve for someone who abused you?

Sometimes, we hold on to the abusive relationship because walking away feels like giving up on the parent, partner, or friendship we hope for. Accepting you won't have this relationship is hard to come to terms with. *But staying doesn't change this.* You need to allow yourself to grieve the loss of the relationship you wish you had, so you can become unbound by the hopes of who they could be.

It is a genuine loss and deserves your grief.

There is also the loss of self to grieve. There is loss of self-identity, loss of self-esteem, and loss of self-worth. Perhaps you feel unsure of your identity other than in connection with the abuser and feel the loss of self-development. There has been loss of friendships and negative effects on physical and mental health. These were experienced throughout the relationship but were masked by its increasing dependence and intensity. So, when the abusive relationship ends, you feel these losses simultaneously.

Not being accepted for who you truly are deserves your grief.

And there is the loss of time. The loss of time spent with the abuser and the time you now take to heal from it.

The loss of time that could have brought you happiness instead of harm deserves your grief.

It is ok to grieve the loss of the abuser. It is ok to grieve the loss of a relationship that was unhealthy. It is ok to grieve for what could have been, even if the reality is not the same as what you're grieving for. It is ok to grieve parts of self you lost along the way and the loss of friendships. It's ok to grieve the loss of time.

It's not only ok; it's necessary.

When you allow yourself to grieve the losses, you are freeing yourself from the inner conflict of being emotionally affected by the loss of someone who hurt you. You are giving yourself permission to feel how you feel, and to feel the pain of loss, which will support you in finding acceptance and peace in the reality.

You are acknowledging your feelings are valid. Which is truly important for healing, because abuse was dedicated to telling you they're not.

Anger

Anger can feel like a forbidden emotion.

One survivor spoke of how she learned to suppress her anger and frustration because whenever she expressed it, it was met with an explosion of rage or the silent treatment. Anger became a taboo emotion for her. She didn't allow herself to feel it, because her anger became associated with her being unworthy of love. This crossed over to other areas of her life.

She was forever being told, 'you have so much patience!' Actually, she wasn't patient, she was numb.

You may have learned when you expressed your own anger it was met with negative consequences and love was withdrawn from you. It taught you to suppress your anger because only positive, agreeable emotions were acceptable and safe. Anger also feels unsafe if it was used as an abusive tool to punish and intimidate you into submission. Or it can feel shameful. We compare our outbursts of anger to the displays of anger from the abuser, which leaves us feeling conflicted or distressed about our own behaviour.

Let me ask you this; why shouldn't you be angry when you have been abused? Your anger is showing you where your boundaries have been violated. You're angry because you know you deserve to be treated better and you want to be treated better. Your anger is telling you abuse is not ok. The more you block out your anger, the more it screams to be heard. Your anger wants you to know you are worthy of love! Your anger is not your enemy.

The negative consequences of anger come when we hold onto, suppress, or express it in negative ways. But allowing yourself to feel your anger is acknowledging the reality of your experiences. This is so important for growth as it helps to reconcile dissonance between how you feel and what you think about the relationship. *I was abused and I feel angry about it!*

Rather than shaming yourself for uncomfortable emotions, hold curiosity as to why you feel them. Ask yourself, what boundary was being crossed? What need was not being met? What triggered my emotion? What do I need in this moment to help me express myself? This will create space for you to process your feelings, find healthy ways to express them, and to implement effective coping mechanisms, so they don't feel so overwhelming.

It is important to process your emotions when you are in a safe space or with trusted people. This is to provide you with support and to protect you from experiencing further harm, where the abuser may use your emotions against you.

Distance

If your environment contains things that affirm the abuser's reality, then the belief in their potential is continuously being strengthened. No wonder the contradiction of what you are being told to believe and what you experienced continues, if you are still receiving external input that tells you the abuser's reality is the 'real truth'. This could be through mutual connections, through news stories or social attitudes, or continued contact with the abuser.

By creating distance between yourself and the things that substantiate your belief in the abuser's reality, it provides you with an uncontaminated space to process your experiences. This enables you to bring congruence to your thoughts and feelings and what you have experienced.

It is not always possible to distance yourself fully, but there are steps you can take to minimise exposure. These include:

Do Not Engage

Do not JADE: justify, argue, defend, or explain yourself to the abuser or others. Do not attack the abuser when others are defending them or try to persuade them of your truth when they are committed to believing the abuser. Their perspective tells you it is not emotionally safe to continue the conversation with them. This will only create greater exposure to the abuser's reality and 'potential', causing further confusion, self-doubt and distress.

You don't have to prove the abuse to anyone. You don't have to deny their experience of the abuser to validate yours, nor do you have to deny your experience to make others comfortable. Neutral statements such as, 'that's your experience but it is not the kind of relationship I have with them', diffuses the need for either of you to justify yourselves. The aim is to end the conversation in a way that is emotionally safe for you. Honouring your experiences, whilst resisting the need to validate them through changing their opinion.

Limit Contact

Do not contact the abuser. This includes looking through their social media pages or finding out information about them through others. Limit your use of social media if others are engaged in a smear campaign and you feel attacked. Block people to protect your mental health if needed. Do not respond to the abuser's attempts to restart an emotional connection. These interactions perpetuate confusion and stoke your belief in their potential, causing further inner conflict.

Shift Focus

Focus on yourself. This might be hard when the loss feels overwhelming, or when there is an active smear campaign. It is ok if you struggle not to ruminate. Just try to create small moments to consciously take a break from your thoughts of past experiences and bring yourself into the present. Whether you choose to journal, take a bath, call a friend, go for a walk, listen to music or to sit and breathe deeply. When you gradually shift focus from the abuser to yourself, it creates space for you to trust in your own truth, believe in yourself, and feel grounded in the present.

Nonconflicting Conclusions

The issue with cognitive dissonance is that by holding conflicting beliefs and thoughts we create inner conflict. With abuse, it's the contrast between the belief and the reality of the relationship with the abuser. We hold opposing thoughts, which result in stress, anxiety, sadness, or regret.

We need to take this process one step further, so we can bring our conflicting thoughts to a nonconflicting conclusion. This will reduce the strength of the old belief and introduce a new belief which aligns with your experiences.

An example would be:

Thought #1 I believe they loved me.

Thought #2 They were abusive towards me whenever I disagreed with them.

Nonconflicting Conclusion: Even if they loved me, their abusive behaviour means it was not a safe relationship for me.

By bringing the two conflicting thoughts together with a nonconflicting conclusion, you are reconciling dissonance and reducing the conflict created between the loving and abusive behaviour. Over time, it reduces the levels of stress, regret, and sadness and takes away its power. Instead, empowering you to find acceptance and peace.

Although it is not a straightforward process to disentangle yourself from the abuser, I have yet to talk to a survivor who said it wasn't worth it. Healing, growth, and peace are on the other side of an abusive relationship.

5 phrases to end the conversation when someone is supporting the abuser:

- o I would like to stop discussing this now.
- o Let's change the subject.
- o Thanks for wanting to talk about it, but I'm not quite ready yet.
- o I'm feeling hurt by this conversation. I would like to talk about something else.
- o I understand how you feel about it, and I still don't feel the same, so let's stop talking about it.

SURVIVOR'S GUIDE

POTENTIAL VERSUS REALITY TAKEAWAYS:

· Idealising behaviours get you hooked on the abuser's potential and the relationship, making it difficult to process the reality of your experiences.

· We form a strong attachment to the belief in the abuser's potential (rather than the reality) through love bombing, a false image of self and future faking, which set up an idealised version of the relationship.

· Red flags are behaviours that leave you feeling something isn't quite right, and include shortcuts to a deep connection, disrespectful behaviours, and inconsistency in what they say versus how they behave.

· An issue with red flags is if we feel disconnected from our intuition, it's difficult to trust it. Or, if red flags are familiar to us, they may not present as a warning. They provide a feeling of safety as we feel safe with familiarity. Therefore, awareness is key.

· The reality of abuse is hard to detect because it increases gradually, meaning you only realise once it is a significant part of the relationship.

· Abuse often increases alongside increased emotional and practical commitments, meaning that as the abuse intensifies, it also becomes more difficult to leave.

· The abuser seeks to maintain power through discarding others when they fear they will be abandoned themselves. They also seek to avoid uncomfortable emotions which arise whilst devaluing you, so seek new opportunities to idealise and avoid their emotions.

· The abuser attempts to maintain your belief in them even after separation, to protect their self-image and public image, and to continue to gain validation through your attention.

· Bringing harmony between the belief and reality of the relationship is key to reducing inner conflict. Allowing yourself to grieve, process your emotions, creating distance and bringing conflicting thoughts to nonconflicting conclusions are ways you can support yourself in restoring balance.

Potential Versus Reality Journal Prompt

Thought One:

Thought Two:

Nonconflicting Conclusion:

Part Four

Breaking the Chains

On average, it takes a woman seven attempts to leave an abusive intimate partner relationship before staying away for good. We've already touched on some reasons. Barriers formed by the abusive behaviour make it extremely difficult to leave the relationship: physically, socially, and financially. Chains formed by the emotional ties to the abuser, feelings of shame, gaslighting and blame-shifting, loss of self, the belief in the relationship, and the unhealthy bond. There is also the increased risk of violence at the point of separation.

This is the tapestry of abuse.

Beyond this, women who speak up about abuse find themselves labelled resentful or crazy, with people preferring to deduce they cannot accept the end of the relationship amicably rather than recognise they are abuse survivors. When you break free from abuse, the last thing you want, need or can cope with is a public lack of understanding.

Yet, these issues are not restricted to women abused by male partners. Men who are abused by female partners experience further shaming through their masculinity being questioned. Or they aren't believed because how could a woman, who is viewed as inherently weaker, abuse a man? One male survivor spoke of how a police officer joked about getting 'beaten by a girl' when he reported abuse. His abuse was minimised, and his experience invalidated when he sought support.

Alternatively, lesbian and bisexual women are less likely to come forward about intimate partner abuse. Not only is abuse itself a hidden experience, but there's a fear that openly discussing abuse in same-sex relationships will generate further negative views when they already face societal prejudices. This is an additional barrier that extends across the LGBTQIA+ community in seeking support after experiencing abuse.

Or in a family setting, when a survivor decides to have no further contact with abusive family members, they are told, 'but she's your mother... he's your father... it's your family, you need to rise above it'. They are shamed, ostracised, and invalidated for removing themselves from experiencing on-going abuse. Someone who was abused as a child should not be told they are cruel for cutting out an abusive parent, rather than recognition of the abusive parent's cruelty. Yet, it happens time and time again.

It is these attitudes towards relationships that hinder us further in breaking the chains, especially when we internalise them. There is stigma around divorce or ending relationships in general, with successful relationships defined by longevity, and loyalty viewed as staying with someone, no matter what happens. These attitudes turn the prospect of ending an abusive relationship into one perceived as a failure, rather than one of safety, growth, and healing. It means ending a relationship with an abuser is one where we face judgement, rather than compassion. We internalise the societal views about love and relationships, which causes us to feel conflicted and ashamed for the 'failure' of the relationship. Yet, these views simply do not apply when you are being abused.

Popular culture also glamorises elements of abusive relationships. The volatile relationship depicted as passionate soulmates. Or the classic storyline of how the love of a good woman tamed an obnoxious lothario, leading to their happy ever after. We are being sold the extreme highs and lows of trauma bonding as the ultimate measure of romance.

All of this contributes to developing thoughts and attitudes about relationships and love that keep you feeling emotionally chained to the abuser. In identifying which of these beliefs you have internalised, you can gain clarity on whether your own attitudes towards love and relationship are negatively affecting you whilst you heal from abuse. This allows you to challenge and reframe your beliefs to support you in your healing.

You have not failed, you have transitioned to safety, and to a desire for healthy relationships.

Understanding what has led to these thoughts, and how they may cause more heartache and discomfort, helps you to let go of unhelpful ideals and develop new beliefs, that support you in building healthy relationships. It is the process of *becoming aware* of your thoughts about the abusive relationship and what you find hard to process. Then, *to acknowledge* how the thought affects your life. How you feel, how it affects you daily or whether it is negatively affecting your well-being and growth. Finally, through recognising how it negatively affects you, it empowers you to take action, to challenge the attitudes you hold and to *facilitate acceptance* of the abusive relationship, for what it is rather than its ideal, as well as a newfound awareness of healthy love for your other relationships.

You deserve a relationship where love is felt, not uttered to excuse abusive behaviour.

Chapter eleven:

Deconstructing Thoughts
(that keep you attached)

In literature, deconstruction is analysing a text to identify contradictions in its meaning. We assume meaning isn't constant, because how a reader interprets a text will change over time, and therefore inconsistencies will be undeniable. I believe this is an important reflection when thinking about relationships. The meaning of a successful relationship changes over time; it changes from childhood through adulthood, as well as across generations. Yet, we often hold on to attitudes from before. When you hold on to attitudes that are inconsistent with your experiences, it hinders growth. You hold expectations of yourself that wouldn't be healthy to strive for in an abusive relationship, such as staying in a marriage 'through the hard times'. This keeps you feeling emotionally chained to the abuser, even though it wasn't a healthy relationship.

To consider deconstructing in a different context, to deconstruct toxic chemicals is to break them down into smaller, non-harmful substances. Deconstructing is taking a substance that's harmful to you and making it safe. This is exactly what we want to achieve with deconstructing our thoughts and attitudes toward the abuser. First, to identify a belief about the relationship that is causing harm by fostering shame, low self-worth, or a lack of acceptance. Then, to break it down so the thoughts no longer hinder your ability to grow, so you can break the chains to the abuser, and go on to have healthier relationships with yourself and others.

Thought: I've Invested so Much!

When you have invested so much of your life, time, energy, and self into the relationship, walking away or accepting the relationship is over feels like losing a significant part of yourself. You invested so much to have the relationship your heart hoped for, and it didn't materialise. *It doesn't seem fair.* There is a sense of regret. And it isn't fair someone took all you gave and choose to harm you.

We are told if we invest all these things, we will gain stable relationships, so when the relationship ends, it feels like a failure and evokes shame. Certain social attitudes towards relationships intensify this feeling. The stigmatisation of divorce or stopping contact with family members. Or the narrative of a successful life following a set timeline, and how we mark a successful relationship by its length, not by mutual happiness. Attitudes of building a successful relationship if we are loyal in marriage, support our parents, and follow traditional timelines, mean we feel the loss of invested time and energy with greater intensity because we didn't get the expected outcome. These attitudes make it harder to break the attachment to the abuser. We long for the success of the relationship we truly believed was possible, rather than to feel the loss of all we have invested.

Sunk Cost Fallacy

When we make a personal investment, such as giving our time, money or other resources, we tend to commit to our decision, even if the negative consequences outweigh the benefits. This is a cognitive bias known as the sunk cost fallacy.

In her book, The Highly Sensitive Person's Guide to Dealing with Toxic People, Shahida Arabi explains how in an abusive relationship, this translates to you continuing to pour yourself into the relationship because of the amount of effort and time you have already invested. Even if you are deeply unhappy. You seek to avoid feeling as though you have wasted everything you have put into the relationship. You believe, 'I've invested 10 years… just one more day might be the day things change'. It creates a vicious cycle because the more you invest, the more committed you feel to the relationship and the greater the challenge to break away from it. You, therefore, stay longer, investing more into the relationship, hoping things will improve, and so the cycle repeats.

Loss Aversion

We are more likely to take a risk to avoid loss than we are for potential gain. This is because we feel loss more acutely than we feel our gains, so our decisions lean towards trying to avoid them. In an abusive relationship, the loss we experience through ending the relationship might feel like a greater threat than the dangers posed by staying. We take the risk of staying with the abuser, not only to avoid the loss of all we have invested, but also parts of our lives we fear the abuser will destroy if we leave. This is even though there is the potential to gain peace of mind, happiness, and healing. After the relationship, an overwhelming sense of loss can make it difficult to process and accept the impact the relationship has had on our lives, so we focus on all we have invested. We replay parts of the relationship, trying to figure out whether things could have been different, *whether we could have invested more*, rather than allowing ourselves to feel the loss of it.

Deconstructing, 'I've Invested so Much'

It's hard to let go of all you have invested because you genuinely loved the abuser and hoped the relationship would be successful. Therefore, the end of the relationship evokes feelings of shame, regret, and a sense of loss. It's a way of holding on to old hope (in the abuser), rather than facing these emotions head on, which will facilitate a path to new hope (in you). Through processing our shame, regret and loss, we deconstruct the thought of how much we have invested and the attachment it creates, empowering us to accept the outcome of the relationship and to shift our investment into ourselves.

Shame

Relationship endings carry shame when we view them as failures. In abusive relationships, shame is intensified through the abuser shifting blame for their behaviour and the end of the relationship onto you. You feel it was your responsibility to make the relationship a success. You made significant sacrifices, yet were rewarded with the breakdown of the relationship. This sense of responsibility means you internalise the failure, viewing yourself as a failure for not helping the abuser to heal, for not making the relationship last, and for investing so much and still losing the future you were trying to build.

This deepens your shame.

We also feel shame when we view separated families as broken homes. In the book Modern Families: Parents and Children in New Family Forms, Susan Golombok discusses how an ideal family unit for healthy child development is built on family bonds, not family structure. It doesn't matter whether you are a family that stayed together, a non-traditional family or a single parent family, what matters most is the relationship you have with your child. Simply knowing this can help ease shame about a 'broken home'. Your home is not broken when you have healthy bonds. You have not failed. It is not too late to feel secure and happy in your home.

To reduce shame, you need to give back responsibility. The breakdown of an abusive relationship is not your fault. It is not because you didn't invest enough. It was not your responsibility to make the abuser stay. You didn't have to change their behaviour or accept abuse as part of the relationship. The success of a relationship is never one person's responsibility. You can give your all and the relationship will not thrive if all the other does is take. Release yourself of the burden of carrying responsibility for their choices.

We remove shame when we stop viewing endings as failures. The relationship with the abuser is not a success just because it continues, neither is it a failure because it ends. A relationship is successful when it's safe, enriching, and develops with mutual intention. Whilst the abuser does not provide these things, the end of the relationship can. The ending is not a failure; it is an opportunity to choose you over a harmful relationship.

When you stop holding yourself to societal relationship milestones, you no longer feel you have failed when you don't achieve them. Often when we compare, we isolate people's relationship successes, according to society, and compare them to our struggles. This compounds the feeling of failure. When you take a significant struggle, such as the end of an abusive relationship, and compare it to someone's relationship highs, you are magnifying the belief you've failed and your sense of shame. No one can uphold all of society's relationship milestones and expectations, yet we feel unworthy because we could not achieve the relationship milestones society holds in high regard.

Shift focus onto honouring your own relationship milestones, which can include endings, and are authentic to your own growth and experiences.

Regret

There is a sense of regret over all the life resources invested into the abuser that now feel wasted. Whilst you cannot change how much you invested into the relationship; you can make the choice to invest in yourself from now on. To take everything you invested into the abuser and work on investing into yourself instead. Your hope, compassion, commitment, time and focus, prioritising needs and valuing opinions, making future plans and *your love*. You've shown great capacity for these in your relationship with the abuser, and you have the ability to transfer all of your belief in them and to place it in yourself, into your healing and your life plans.

When you place hope in the abuser, gently remind yourself it is your healing that is worthy of your hope. When you value their opinion above your own, acknowledge your opinion of yourself is of greater value than someone who harmed you. The more you invest in yourself now, the less regret you will feel over investing in the abuser in the past.

Remember, it is the abuser who wasted the opportunity to have a healthy relationship with you, not you who wasted time for investing in something you believed in.

Loss

It is important not to bypass the loss of an abusive relationship. It might also be the loss of your ideal family unit or the lifelong relationship you longed for and placed significant hope in. Losing the relationship might feel like losing your one shot at happiness. When your sense of worth is connected to your 'one shot', it will be deeply affected by the loss. You might fear you will always be alone without the abuser, and therefore, your loss feels even greater. Allow yourself to sit, rest and feel grief for the loss and harm you endured.

Alongside processing loss, you can also ground yourself in the present in small and significant ways. Being aware of not having to walk on eggshells or evade the abuser's unpredictable moods. Being able to leave the lights on without someone flying into a rage. Staying in your jogging pants all day if you want to. Making decisions without having to think through every plausible scenario of how they may interpret and react to it. Being able to release tension in your body, to sit calmly and simply exhale. Recognising the small freedoms in your daily life supports you in building a life around the loss, rather than feeling engulfed by it.

Thought: I Believe in the Good in Them!

Once upon a time there was a successful, charismatic, (albeit chauvinistic), young man.

One night, he finds himself stranded in the middle of nowhere. He wanders to a small nearby village into the local pub. There he talks to a girl-next-door type of woman who works behind the bar.

It's as though their paths were destined to cross.

She is kind, naturally funny, and shows him empathy for his predicament. However, instead of seeing her inherent worth, the young man is all shades of obnoxious towards her, believing her to be small worldly and beneath him with her humble lifestyle.

Nonetheless, over the following weeks, with just the right mixture of patience, loyalty, compassion and zest for life, the girl-next-door thaws the young man's frosty temperament to bring his good-hearted nature to the forefront.

Just how she saw his true goodness within, he realises her true beauty, and they live,

Happily.

Ever.

After.

Popular culture is saturated with stories of romance that centre on one person's good nature helping the other to find the goodness within themselves. It's not just romance. It's also the absent parent, who cannot see the inherent worth of their child because they are dissatisfied with their life and focused on chasing success. However, they come to realise through the innocent joy of their child, that their life is already successful. This allows them to step up to be the parent their child deserves.

This message is harmful in abusive relationships. It gives a false sense of control over the outcome of someone else's behaviour. It's the girl-next-door's love or child's purity that rescues someone from themselves, saving the relationship. We therefore believe if we were good enough, if we were 'the one', we could break down their walls. When the abuse continues, rather than hold the abuser accountable, you believe it's your love that isn't worthy. If you could love them enough and love them the right way, you could help them return to the goodness within and have the relationship you hope for.

The only person who can make that choice is the abuser themselves.

We unconsciously learn that if we are worthy, the goodness in the abuser will prevail. This is a dangerous belief to internalise because it leads to self-blame, shame and is destructive to our self-worth. When they continue to abuse you, even though you have tried your best, you believe it is because you aren't enough. *No amount of loving someone is going to eradicate or change their abusive behaviour.* That doesn't change with love. It changes with self-reflection, accountability, desire to change, and immense commitment. You are not in control of their behaviour, actions or choices. Connecting the quality of your love to their behaviour, simultaneously connects your sense of worth to the outcome. When they continue to abuse, your belief in your ability to love and be loved suffers.

Moreover, when you believe in the good in them, it provides you with hope the relationship will improve. This is another belief that keeps us attached to harmful relationships. We don't want to give up on them, so we stay and wait for their goodness to prevail. Or after the relationship has ended, we struggle to let go because we believe in their goodness.

Fairy Tale Romance

Some survivors of abuse fantasise about the fairy tale romance. The fairy tale romance soothes wounds such as feeling unseen, unworthy, unloved, or abandoned. However, when you fantasise about romance, you are more susceptible to the abuser's love bombing and relationship idealisations because these attend to your wounds, in the short term. The abuser strides into your life as the rescuer, saving you from the hurt of past wounds.

When we romanticise someone, we give ourselves the feeling they are safe without getting to know them or acknowledging who they are. We attach to the fantasy with them rather than the reality and therefore give ourselves the feeling it is safe to love them. When the abuser devalues you, however, you inadvertently end up in a similar role you previously experienced, with your needs unmet and your wounds unattended to. Instead of the relationship rescuing you from past hurt, it becomes a source of re-experiencing your past wounds.

You may also feel a responsibility to become the rescuer, saving the relationship and the abuser from themselves. When you are unable to rescue them, it is you that feels shame for the fracture of the fairy tale romance.

Reverse Projection

I've heard someone diagnosed with narcissistic personality disorder say, 'if you are that easy to manipulate, then it's shame on you, not shame on me.'

Not everyone will share your morals.

Not everyone will share your values.

Not everyone will share your belief of what defines the good in someone.

The abuser may very well consider themselves to be in touch with their goodness. Their morals and values might not align with yours. If so, your description of goodness isn't something they desire to adhere to. It won't even be on their radar, and if you bring it to their attention, they will not agree with you their behaviour is abusive. Abusers believe they have a right to superior treatment. Or they believe their behaviour is perfectly acceptable because they are not physically abusive. Therefore, any attempt to get them in touch with your definition of goodness will be utterly fruitless.

Reverse projection is when you project your positive attributes onto another. An example is, because you value honesty, you believe the abuser also values honesty and is authentic in their communication, even with evidence to the contrary. The issue with reverse projection is the goodness you see in the abuser is a projection of your own qualities. You stay attached to the abuser or give them repeated chances because you believe the good you see *is in them*, rather than recognising it is your own qualities you have projected onto them.

Waiting for the 'Old Them'

Waiting for the old them is similar to believing in the good. Whereas the premise of believing in the good is we are all good-natured at our core, the difficulty with waiting for the 'old them' is you believe you have concrete examples in your past where the abuser was a different version of themselves. This makes the prospect of them returning to the old version more realistic, as you aren't hoping they become someone they're not, you are hoping for them to become someone they used to be.

It is hard to accept the end of the relationship because of the uncertainty of whether the abuser could return to the 'old them'. It can lead to further shame, if you feel you gave up on them and could not restore the relationship to the 'good times.' When we understand there is no good and bad version, and see the abuser whole, we break the attachment to the 'old them'. It empowers us to recognise the highs and lows of idealisation and devaluation as part of their behavioural patterns, rather than fixed parts of their character we can return to with any sense of stability.

Deconstructing, 'I believe in the Good in Them'

Being a romantic is nothing to be ashamed of; it doesn't signal naivety. What it shows is your propensity for kindness and your heart's desire to experience love. When you haven't felt loved, you are more compelled to look to movie standards of love, and these can be unrealistic and unhealthy. Daydreaming about true love and the love of fairy tales blinds us to the bad, the abusive and simply the incompatible. When someone shows us their bad, or abusive behaviour, we magnify their goodness, as it is painful to realise it won't be the relationship we hope for. We look to soothe our wounds of feeling unloved or unseen through finding our soulmate. Yet, we end up in relationships where we feel invisible again.

Healing wounds

When you heal the wounds fairy tale love attends to, it lessens the urgency of meeting these needs in new relationships and therefore the desire to see the good in others. We want to believe they are good because we seek to heal our old wounds in new relationships. In abusive relationships, this feeling is intensified through trauma bonding, as you look to the abuser to heal the pain they caused.

When you begin to heal your wounds, you are no longer dependent on the abuser's goodness to comfort you. This helps to break the attachment to the good in the abuser. You can let go of the need to see good in them because you no longer look to them to heal your pain.

This creates space to explore and define healthy relationships. Ask yourself, what type of connection am I looking for? How do I feel safe in my relationships? What provides me with stability and happiness? What actions through the day help me to feel loved? *Were these fulfilled in the relationship I had with them?* This supports you in recognising the unhealthy relationship with the abuser, regardless of whether they are capable of goodness. It also empowers you to enter new relationships with greater clarity. Rather than longing to be loved and romanticising new relationships, you can enter them with, yes, a desire to love and be loved, but also a greater awareness of how you want your relationship to progress and how you actually define love.

Believe in what they show you

The abuser's potential for good is immaterial when you have to live with the reality of abuse. Importantly, their inability to function in and form healthy relationships has nothing to do with your worth or the quality of your love. Believe the abuser when they repeatedly treat you abusively. It doesn't matter whether they have good in them, what matters is the relationship you have with them.

Whether the relationship is safe for you.

5 reflections for success in relationships:

- o Supports development and personal growth.
- o A safety to show up authentically. To be able to express yourself openly in the relationship and be accepted for who you are.
- o Where happiness is prioritised over longevity.
- o Honouring individual (not societal) relationship milestones.
- o Fighting the problem, not fighting each other.

Thought: What if They Change?

The possibility of change is always going to cause a lingering attachment. The niggling doubt that if you held on for one more day, there might be a turning point and a chance for the relationship to blossom into a success. The problem is, the abuser doesn't see fault in the way they treated you. They have justified, reasoned, buried, and made excuses for themselves to find their behaviour acceptable. They feel entitled, believing it necessary for the greater good (their needs). Or they blame you, convinced your shortcomings initiated their actions.

And if they see no fault, they see no reason to change.

Acknowledgement

A majority of abusers do not acknowledge their behaviour as abusive. Without acknowledgement, there is no change.

There may be fleeting moments of acknowledgment that are quickly shrouded in denial or justification to protect their ego. With longer term acknowledgment, the abuser rationalises and minimises their behaviour to find it acceptable. Or they place blame elsewhere. It is notoriously difficult for abusers to change, as they have an external locus of control, meaning they blame you, others, or what's happening around them for their abusive behaviour. Any acknowledgement, therefore, lacks accountability. They do not take responsibility for their behaviour or acknowledge the full extent of harm it has caused.

They neither see a need to change or for it to be in their power to do so.

Some abusers see their behaviour harms you, and still have no desire to change because they benefit from the current situation. If they are driven to self-serve and lack a moral conscience about causing others harm, then their best choice is to continue with their behaviour. Why would they want to change?

In their eyes, it's you who has the problem, or you who is the problem.

Accountability

The reason we often hear 'abusers never change' is because most abusers do not successfully integrate accountability for their behaviour into their understanding of themselves to make effective and long-lasting change.

However, accountability alone isn't enough to see effective change. There needs to be a strong desire to do it. Changing deep-rooted behavioural patterns and belief systems takes dedication and long-term commitment. If the abuser comes to you after a month and says, 'I've changed', it's simply not a possibility. There may be an intention, but is it a genuine commitment to change, or is it a response to losing their hold over you that will fade away once you step back into the dynamic? Usually, any vow to change is short term. It is an attempt to self-soothe when there is an increase of vulnerable emotions, and an attempt to regain a sense of power and control over the relationship.

Established Dynamic

If the abuser has acknowledged the full extent of their behaviour, holds themselves accountable and is committed to change, then you need to consider that there is already an unhealthy relationship dynamic established between you. They are more likely to fall into old habits of abusive behaviours where abuse was previously part of the dynamic. You aren't starting with a clean slate; you are restarting with a history of abuse. How you both interact with one another is already affected by the control and power dynamic and abusive patterns of behaviour. So, there is additional work to alter how they behave *specifically towards you*, so as not to fall into 'old habits.' Whilst this is not impossible, it is important to keep in mind change doesn't happen overnight and there will almost certainly be times where you experience further abuse, even if they commit to change.

Consider your safety and the affect this will have on you.

And... So, What if They Change?

Often, we romanticise the idea of the abuser changing. We believe it will be the key to unlocking our happy-ever-after relationship. It hurts because it feels like a change would solve everything... but it's out of our control. In reality, it is more complex. Would you be able to create safety in a relationship that has been incredibly unsafe for you? Would you be able to build a connection where you thrive? Would you also get the support you need to process and heal from their abusive behaviour? Would change even give you the relationship you hope for, or are you longing for a relationship that simply doesn't exist with this person?

Deconstructing, 'What if They Change?'

Deconstructing, 'what if they change', brings us to questions beneath the question. What we are really asking is, 'what does it mean if they change after the relationship has ended?' In breaking down the thoughts attached to this question, you can find acceptance in the relationship outcome. Instead of your peace being affected by whether the abuser changes, this empowers you to find peace and acceptance from within.

Did I give up too soon?

Choosing safety is not giving up on a relationship. Even if the abuser commits to change, there is no obligation for you to stay in an unsafe environment whilst they work on their behaviour. If they are authentic in the acknowledgment and accountability of their abuse, they will understand your choice to remove yourself from an unsafe relationship whilst they do the inner work. Otherwise, it sounds a lot like more manipulation.

Chances are, however, the abuser will not commit long-term to change and you did everything you could to make the relationship work. It is not your duty to continuously self-sacrifice. The abuser has a responsibility to change their abusive behaviour to maintain the relationship. It is not your responsibility to remain in an unsafe relationship to maintain it.

Am I the cause of the abuse?

There is a fear if they change in a new relationship, then you caused their abusive behaviours. This echoes the abuser's mentality of, 'it is you with the problem or you who is the problem'. Survivors internalise this message, especially when they see the abuser appears to change in a new relationship. It reinforces the belief abuse was only present with you, and therefore, it was because of you.

Nothing could be further from the truth. We KNOW the abuser is responsible for their own behaviour. Not you. And yet, do you FEEL this? When you see them in a new relationship, looking as though they've changed, do you still ask yourself, *'was I the problem?'* Sometimes, we don't get answers. Sometimes, no matter how in depth an answer is, it only leads to more questions. Sometimes, simple answers can be enough to facilitate acceptance.

Here is the simple answer: looks can be deceiving.

Think about how your relationship appeared to others and whether anyone knew the full extent of what was happening. The abuser presents an image of the relationship they want the outside world to see. The likelihood is, they have not changed. They have carried the same patterns and behaviours into the next relationship, hidden from view.

Could I have had the relationship I hoped for?

This is again an attachment to the potential rather than the relationship itself. The potential of the relationship directly soothes the pain of the reality by providing hope. The reality is you felt unloved and unseen by the abuser, but the potential is you could be loved and seen if they changed. Ultimately, the hope of change prolongs the attachment. It's hard to let go because you genuinely love them and want the relationship to be a success.

Shifting focus onto yourself supports you in letting go of the hope they could change. Choosing yourself over a harmful relationship, placing hope in your healing instead of in the abuser changing, and seeing the abuser for who they currently are, not who they have the potential to become. This perspective gives you autonomy over the direction of your life, whereas placing hope in the abuser's ability to change gives them power over your happiness. When they have treated your happiness with such little regard until now, is it worth placing your continued happiness in their hands?

Instead of focusing on the relationship you hoped for with the abuser, focus on building a relationship you hope for with yourself.

This also lessens the fear of the abuser changing in a new relationship. When you heal, it becomes inconsequential. It doesn't matter whether the abuser is different in a new relationship because they were abusive towards you. When you give back ownership of the abuse to the abuser, this is less threatening to acknowledge, because you truly accept the abuse was not your fault.

Their behaviour is their responsibility.

Thought: They Aren't Always Abusive!

The thought they aren't always abusive feeds into the self-doubt survivors have about their perception of the abuse. You worry you might have judged them too harshly, overreacted or your expectations in the relationship were too high. These doubts are frequently reinforced when survivors share their story with others, due to a lack of social understanding of the nuances of abuse. When you open up to someone about your experiences and they respond to your vulnerability with, 'they are just having a hard time' or, 'they've always been kind to me', it throws you back into the cycle of doubting your perception, making it harder to break away from the attachment.

Certain attitudes such as 'nobody's perfect' or 'relationships are hard work', cause further confusion when you are trying to determine whether they are abusive. Whilst it may be true and said with good intentions, these attitudes can create unhealthy expectations in abusive relationships, that keep you bound to the abuser. Combined with worn down self-trust, you wonder whether you've labelled normal relationship highs and lows as abusive, adding to the shame of not having tried harder or the regret of the relationship ending.

Jekyll and Hyde

Like the man who was inflicted with two personas in Robert Louis Stevenson's novella of the kind-hearted Dr Jekyll and evil Mr Hyde, the abuser's kind and abusive behaviour is so contrasting, they seem like two different people. The problem is, you never know if you are going to get Jekyll or Hyde. The unpredictability of their behaviour not only leads to hypervigilance and living in constant survival mode but also provides a glimmer of hope. There is hope for their kind-hearted nature to overpower their abusive tendencies. More than this, the interjection of positive interactions causes you to question the severity of their abuse. The good days clouding your understanding of how abusive they are. Was it just a slip up? Did they really mean it? Maybe it's not that bad...? This enters you into the cycle of doubting your boundaries and response to their abuse, rather than seeing clearly that their abusive behaviour is unacceptable.

Thinking of how they aren't always abusive continues the attachment, as you question whether the relationship was as bad as you perceived. Ultimately, we hope 'they aren't always abusive', will lead to, 'they are never abusive'. Or perhaps you wonder, were they ever, really? This leads to doubt in your decision to protect yourself through detaching from the relationship. Rather than feeling confident the relationship was harmful, you feel conflicted by their Jekyll and Hyde behaviour.

Public Persona

When you see how capable the abuser is of warmth towards others, it does two things.

First, you draw the conclusion, if they are kind towards others, you must be the problem. You believe you must cause their behaviour. You must be provoking them, you must be difficult, you must be too sensitive, needy, selfish, and all the things they say you are. *This deeply affects self-worth.* The person you long to share a loving connection with is providing it to others and denying it to you. We believe we must be inherently unworthy of love and warmth, because others receive the abuser's kindness with ease.

Second, this leads to you trying to prove your worth. Instead of feeling enough as you are, you try to please and appease the abuser by bending yourself in all shapes and directions, with the hope they will reward you with the warmth and kindness they show to others. It's similar to the good times clouding judgement of how the bad times are abusive. The trap of thinking, 'they aren't abusive to others' is overriding the fact they abuse you, because it provides hope that they can show you similar warmth and kindness.

When considering why abusers are kind to others and abusive in the home, it's helpful to remember it doesn't serve them to be abusive all the time. Part of an abusive mentality is to manipulate, so often, the non-abusive behaviour is self-serving as well. When others think highly of the abuser, it boosts their ego, reinforces the image of who they want to be and helps them to reason their abusive behaviour towards you. It also deepens the power imbalance. Where you feel more isolated, misunderstood and invalidated, the abuser feels more self-righteous in their behaviour and position of authority.

Abusers do not have the same control and attachment in all their relationships, so to abuse people beyond their primary relationships would be to lose the power, status or image they hold. Showing abusive behaviour would weaken their position of power, not strengthen it. Therefore, the optimal way to maintain power is to present a façade. People become so attached to the abuser's façade, even if they see abusive behaviour towards you, they justify, minimise and enable it. The façade becomes part of the fabric of abuse. It allows the abuser to manipulate their public image and avoid accountability, whilst channelling their gaslighting, invalidation, and abusive behaviour through other people. This is how abusers maintain control through their public persona.

So yes, it is true the abuser isn't abusive towards everyone, but to break this chain, we can remember:

1. It does not minimise their abusive behaviour towards you.

2. The non-abusive behaviour with others is self-serving in the same way abusive behaviour is self-serving with you. In this sense, the non-abusive behaviour is manipulative and part of their abusive mindset.

3. It is not a reflection of your worth; it is a protection of their image.

Deconstruct, 'They Aren't Always Abusive'

The abuser thrives on compartmentalising parts of self and their behaviour. They get you to view their abuse as isolated incidents and limited to specific people or situations, rather than viewing it as pattern of their behaviour and wider manipulation. This keeps you attached to the parts of them that aren't abusive and the hope of situations that don't lead to abuse.

Integration

Integrating the abuser's kind and abusive behaviour, to view them as a whole, will help to break the attachment to them not being abusive all the time. It supports you in recognising abuse is a pattern of their behaviour and therefore part of the relationship.

A simple therapeutic technique to integrate all of their behaviour into your understanding of the relationship, is to replace BUT with AND in your thinking.

For Example:

Instead of: 'They were threatening to hurt me today BUT they told me they loved me yesterday.'

Say: 'They were threatening to hurt me today AND they told me they loved me yesterday.'

The BUT unintentionally minimises or excuses abusive behaviour. It leads you to question whether their loving words cancel out the abuse. Whereas, when you reflect on their behaviour thinking AND, it integrates the experience of them as abusive and kind, without their positive behaviour justifying or minimising the abuse. This will help you process abuse within the relationship without the thought of 'they aren't always abusive', clouding your perception of it. Through integration, you can make decisions for yourself with greater clarity rather than feeling confused and remaining attached to their non-abusive behaviour.

5 things you gain when an abusive relationship ends:

- o **Clarity of Your Thoughts:** The confusion and mental exhaustion from abuse subsides and you gain clarity on your truth and experiences.
- o **Self-Trust:** You trust yourself and can build healthier relationships as you learn to trust others and your intuition.
- o **Letting Your Guard Down:** You can relax, exhale and rest. You can feel your feelings, speak your mind, and be in your environment without walking on eggshells.
- o **Inner Peace:** Being away from inconsistent, unpredictable, and abusive behaviour supports you in building a sense of safety and inner peace.
- o **Self-Worth:** As your self-worth grows, you believe you deserve better, and make choices that bring you joy and give you hope.

Chapter twelve:

Redefining Love

If unhealthy relationships are all you've known, then healthy love can leave you feeling exposed, smothered, and uncomfortable. Redefining love is empowering because it is acknowledging you don't have to accept relationships that hurt you.

If you grew up in a home which was volatile, emotionally disconnected or chaotic and this was labelled love, then your tolerance for instability will be higher. You may not regard a lack of safety and consistency as a lack of love. You might repeat unhealthy relationships, because rather than seeing abusive behaviour as a red flag, it has been integrated into the concept of love. It's what love looks and feels like from your experiences, even if it isn't what you imagine when you think about love.

Often, abusers will hold immature beliefs about love, which feed into the abusive dynamic. This is part of the abusive narrative, of course, because it allows them to avoid accountability or to reflect on the reality of their behaviour. How much easier it is to justify their behaviour if they can hurt you and say they did it in the name of love. How much harder it is to break away from the abuser, or to believe you can have a relationship free from abuse, if you have learned this is how love feels.

Many attitudes towards love, which are widespread in society, make it that much harder to gain clarity when trying to process abuse. Attitudes such as, 'love is all you need', or 'love conquers all', clearly have good intent, but can be harmful when you are trying to break the emotional attachment to an abuser. They do not apply to abusive relationships, yet you may have internalised these beliefs, which become a source of inner conflict, turmoil, and shame.

Love can only remain stable in a healthy environment. When you apply these beliefs to an unhealthy relationship, loving the other person requires us to lack in love for ourselves. Part of growth is to tease apart the abusive narrative from your own ideas and values, and to recognise that abuse and love are separate. To reflect on socially accepted attitudes towards love and to be brave and reject the ones that don't apply to your experiences, so you can form beliefs that bring you inner peace and clarity.

Redefining love, so that loving someone else isn't at the cost of self-love.

Love Hurts

A survivor told me, her abusive ex-husband justified his behaviour to their children by saying, 'sometimes love hurts'. The children had witnessed him tell their mother he was going to smash her face in and call the police if she used the car to leave (because it belonged to him). They heard him tell her, without him, she will be homeless on the streets, and when it happens, he will be standing over her laughing. Over the course of the next month, she left him with their children. His response was to write them a letter which read, amongst other things, 'sometimes love hurts.' Months later, her 6-year-old daughter asked how old she had to be to learn to drive. When her mother asked why, she replied, 'because when I'm older I want to have my own car so I can leave whenever I want'.

Normalising Abuse

When someone says love hurts as an explanation for abuse, it is gaslighting. They are leading you to question your perception of what abuse and love feel like. It's like holding a rotten apple in the hand and saying, 'look, a ripe apple! This apple is good, this apple is healthy, this apple will give you nutrients.' It denies the truth of the matter, which is that the apple is rotten. Whereas you may have once said, 'this is a rotten apple' over time you ask, 'is it really rotten, or is this just what apples are like?'

This is the process of how abuse becomes normalised. Rather than being able to identify abusive behaviour, the lines become blurred, and abuse is integrated into your perception of a loving relationship. Not only does it teach you love and abuse can co-exist, but it may have taught you abuse IS love. Abuse is what love looks like. Abuse is how love feels. Have you ever caught yourself thinking, 'they only lose their temper because they care so much about me', or 'they only get jealous when I go out because they worry about me.' This is abusive and controlling behaviour that has been normalised through the idea that, sometimes, love hurts.

Safety Feels Loveless

Love hurts teaches you to equate your nervous system being triggered to how being in love feels, and this is partly why a safe relationship can feel loveless. We misread the intense activation of fight or flight as an intensity of love, rather than identifying abusive behaviour as the cause. This can lead to a vulnerability for volatile relationships, as there is a need for intense emotions and heightened responses because we recognise it as love.

Simultaneously, we feel numb in safe relationships, as our calm nervous system is mistaken for a lack of love. When healing from abuse, it is safe relationships that might feel most uncomfortable. As you transition from the abusive narratives of love to being able to accept and embrace healthy love, you might feel on edge in the calmness, your body prepared to jump into survival mode, and your mind unsettled by what it means for your love connection.

Reframe: Love Is Safe

Relationships aren't void of difficult times, challenging emotions or unhealthy behaviours but there is a safety that is consistent throughout. Love allows for you to be open and emotionally vulnerable. Where abuse takes your vulnerabilities and uses them to gain advantage, love sees your vulnerabilities and holds them with care.

When it isn't safe, it isn't love.

Vulnerability includes sharing your opinions, expressing your emotions, striving for personal goals, and making decisions. It also includes being able to have disagreements or admitting when you are struggling. These things may seem simple to others, but abuse teaches us it is unsafe to be open, so there is vulnerability in allowing ourselves to share who we are with others. Loving relationships, however, won't use parts of who you are against you.

The difficulty for survivors is allowing themselves to be vulnerable to experience safe love. If trusting another was unsafe for you, or conflict has previously led to abuse, you might pre-empt it and therefore not allow yourself to be vulnerable in your relationships as self-protection.

It is also preventing you, though, from being openly you and loved for who you are.

It is through experiences such as having conflict resolved compassionately, receiving an authentic apology, and someone accepting your feelings, that you gradually build evidence it is safe to trust people with your emotions when the relationship is healthy.

Here are three signs someone is safe to trust with your emotional vulnerability:

Emotional Maturity

Emotional maturity is the ability to express yourself appropriately with a good level of emotional control. Emotionally mature people are aware of their emotions and can take ownership of their behaviour. Whilst they may have emotional outbursts, with discernment you can recognise these outbursts don't make you feel unsafe. They apologise authentically, do not use your past behaviour against you, and take action to communicate their feelings productively. They are respectful of other's emotions whilst understanding they are not responsible for the emotions of others.

Emotional Availability

Emotional availability enables healthy connections in a relationship to be sustained. Emotionally available people are attuned to their own emotions and willing to express them, which enables them to be consistent and reliable in their behaviour, attempt to communicate openly and with a sense of togetherness to overcome issues. Their words and actions align, and they show consideration for your emotions and boundaries. They can compromise, remain respectful, and make plans with you, taking steps to follow through.

Constancy

Constancy in relationships provides security through periods of harmony and friction. The status of the relationship isn't thrown into question every time there are tensions. People who are emotionally constant will not threaten abandonment in response to conflict.

Unconditional Love

Unconditional love in an abusive dynamic becomes a one-sided, unconditional relationship. The reason for this is, it's not about love, it's about power and control. The abuser uses the notion of unconditional love to avoid having to address their abusive behaviour, stating that if you loved them, you would accept them as they are. Notice the blame shift, that it is your lack of love and acceptance rather than the abuse that causes relationship issues. This may be a conscious manipulation or a genuine belief, stemming from their sense of entitlement and denial about their abusive behaviour. The abuser feels entitled to behave how they choose, with the expectation you should accept it without question.

The double standard is, whilst you are expected to love them unconditionally, the abuser expects you to meet countless conditions just to receive kindness. These conditions are unsustainable, so when you inevitably fail, their love, affection, and warmth are withdrawn as punishment.

Unconditional Tolerance

The abuser's interpretation of unconditional love is you should unconditionally tolerate abuse. Because they have equated love to tolerance, they can justify to themselves you are in the wrong if you find their behaviour unacceptable. For them, if you will not tolerate their behaviour, then you do not love them. It is an easier process to discard you and blame your lack of tolerance, ahem, I mean 'love', as the reason for the breakdown of the relationship than to take ownership for their abusive behaviour.

If you have learned to equate the quality of your love with how much you will tolerate, there is a deep sense of shame when you finally say, 'enough, I can't take this anymore'. If you have learned your love is only good enough when you forgo personal boundaries, this leads to further shame and confusion when you attempt to set healthy boundaries and no longer tolerate abuse. You might feel you are applying conditions to them receiving your love, in the same way they have applied conditions on you.

Actually, conditions and boundaries are not the same.

Conditions versus Boundaries

Conditions = focused on changing the other person

Conditions lack in accepting someone for who they are (or a situation). They focus on moulding another through withholding relationship needs, such as attention and affection, to gain a desired outcome. The person making conditions may be concerned with how others affect their image, as they worry how they will be perceived through association. Conditions allow for the person setting them to continue with unhealthy attitudes rather than self-reflect and address them. Conditions negatively affect wellbeing because they either reject parts of you, disregard boundaries or invalidate your responses. It leads to feelings of unworthiness.

Conditions are usually about protecting ego rather than wellbeing.

Boundaries = focused on protecting your wellbeing

With boundaries, we accept someone for who they are, whilst expecting they (and ourselves) uphold fundamental relationship values. These include respect, honesty, and equality. Boundaries protect your wellbeing and support you in maintaining healthy relationships. They do not negatively affect another's wellbeing as they are not a rejection of them but a protection of yourself. Boundaries focus on building a healthy environment through your own choices, rather than trying to mould another. With children, boundaries are not an attempt to change them, but a guide to support them in their development and provide them with safety in the home. Relationship needs are not withdrawn when boundaries are crossed, although there can be valid consequences. They sound like, 'I feel uncomfortable when someone shouts at me, so I can only continue the conversation if you are able to stop shouting.'

If someone reacts negatively to your boundary, it's because of what they bring to the table. That's work they need to do, not you.

As with emotionally and psychologically abusive behaviour, it is a pattern of setting conditions that equates to conditional love and emotional harm. Further, it is a valid consequence of abuse or repeated boundary violations to end a relationship or have no further contact. This is not the same as withholding relationship needs.

Reframe: Love with Boundaries

Whilst you may have learned boundaries are selfish, they are in fact, a part of love.

Loving to Self

Foremost, boundaries are loving towards yourself. You deserve love! You are not selfishly prioritising *your wants*; boundaries support you in meeting *your needs*. Boundaries are a tool for you to uphold your values in life and in your relationships. Not only do they support you in maintaining your wellbeing through how your relationships develop, but they also support you in maintaining your wellbeing through your relationship with yourself.

When you learn to set boundaries, you also learn you are a safe person *for yourself*. This will increase your levels of self-trust because you are prioritising yourself instead of self-abandoning, which will also increase your self-esteem.

Loving to Others

Boundaries are loving towards others. Yes, it is loving to set boundaries with people! Boundaries provide clear communication and when it is a healthy relationship, this allows for the other person to love you, with consideration of your boundaries, and to avoid unintentionally hurting you. Boundaries provide the parameters of how to connect harmoniously with one another. When we don't communicate our boundaries, it has negative effects on healthy relationships because it leads to feelings of resentment towards the other person.

Children, who need unconditional parental love for healthy emotional development, thrive with boundaries. Of the four parenting styles, authoritative is optimal in developing resilience, independence and social competency in children. An authoritative parenting style is nurturing with clear guidance, which is essentially, love with boundaries. The other three parenting styles are:

Permissive: nurturing and lacking in boundaries.

Neglectful: lacking in nurture and in boundaries.

Authoritarian: lacking in nurture with high expectations and inflexible rules.

Although different parenting styles may lend themselves to different situations or child temperaments, the take-home message is that the best environment for a child's emotional development in one with unconditional love AND boundaries. This helps us to understand boundaries are a part of loving relationships and it is true for our adult relationships, too. In her book, Set Boundaries, Find Peace, Nedra Glover Tawwab discusses how boundaries facilitate healthy relationships. Without them, we tend to neglect self-care, and feel overwhelmed, resentful and avoid uncomfortable situations. With them, we feel safe, loved, calm and respected. It's not selfish, it's loving.

5 boundaries in relationships:

- o **Communication:** how you respond to disrespectful communication, how frequently you talk to them, when and how to disengage from the conversation, what information you share with them (are they a safe person).
- o **Personal:** forms of self-care such as resting when you need to, taking time for yourself and saying no to things that drain you. It also includes keeping to a budget, practising positive self-talk, and being conscious of content you consume (social media or information received through others).
- o **Time:** setting realistic goals, holding realistic expectations, allowing for rest, asking for help, and sharing responsibilities with others.
- o **Emotional:** allowing yourself to cry, spending time with people who are good for your emotional wellbeing, sharing personal experiences with people who validate your emotions, and removing yourself from stressful situations.
- o **Space:** honouring your right to have personal space, how you respond if someone reads through your phone or journal without permission, respecting other's right for privacy, and only hugging or having physical closeness when you feel comfortable, not pressured.

All You Need Is Love

When we think of all you need is love, we think of compassion diffusing disagreements. How love can overcome any conflict. We think of the belief, if we show kindness in the face of rage, love will conquer. The danger is, not everyone is a safe person to love. This belief in love may have led to many times of showing compassion in the face of abuse, only to be subjected to more. You cannot love the abuser into being kind.

The crucial element to consider is the abuser's mentality. Whilst they hold an abusive mindset, they will absorb your love and use it to further manipulate and abuse you. Love is not all you need to keep you safe. It isn't the magic ingredient to a healthy and happy relationship. And it won't be the catalyst to change the abuser's unhealthy patterns. That has to come from within them.

In an abusive relationship, the abuser can use 'all you need is love' to shun their responsibilities whilst simultaneously implying your needs *beyond love* are a burden. An abusive parent has a responsibility to provide for their child, and excuses their neglect with, 'isn't my love enough for you?' An abusive partner has a responsibility to abide by the boundaries of the relationship, such as monogamy or not spending all your joint savings, and responds to repeated violations with, 'but I love you', as if this is all you should need and expect. Or repeatedly letting you down. Broken promises. Forgotten commitments. These are all relationship responsibilities that seem to dissipate into thin air because of the words, 'I love you.'

When you attempt to hold the abuser to their responsibilities, they shift focus by labelling your needs as demanding or ungrateful. They blame your needs as unacceptable rather than their lack of consideration for your needs, and their abuse. Abusers put minimal effort into the relationship, and then proclaim, 'why do you always need more?!' The idea that love should be enough, not only justifies the abuser's lack of effort, but also causes you to feel shame for needing more. This builds a relationship where your needs are not only disregarded, but you feel it's unreasonable to have them.

The abuser's needs, however, are central in both your minds.

It's Ok to Have Needs

After abuse, you might feel you always have to be 'chill' in your relationships. You want others to see you as relaxed, easy-going, up for a laugh, and able to go with the flow, otherwise you worry about being labelled uptight or high maintenance. This is a response to feeling as though your needs are a burden. Being told you are smothering when you look for affection, or you are too clingy, too needy, too sensitive, or too much, may have left you feeling unable to accept not only your needs, but yourself. Simply asking for anything causes anxiety as to whether you're asking for too much.

Having needs doesn't make you needy. It makes you human.

We ALL have relationship needs. Period. There's a need to belong, for authentic connection, and to be seen and heard. A need for safety. A need to develop and grow. We have a need for affection, understanding and for compromise. We seek to face problems together, not against one another, and to repair through honest communication. We need clarity in our relationships. *We need happiness and satisfaction in our relationships.* And we need to feel competent and empowered about our life choices. We can't have our needs met all the time, but it is normal and healthy to have them. It isn't demanding. It isn't ungrateful. It isn't too much. There isn't something inherently wrong with you for needing more than love.

Reframe: Love Enriches Fulfilling Relationships

We can recognise love is enriching AND it is not enough alone. Relationships need a baseline. Without one, they become chaotic and unstable.

Think of your relationship as a house, and love as its beauty. You can pour all of your effort into making the most beautiful home and yet if you have built it upon sand, it will sink. A house needs more than beauty, it needs firm foundations. Relationships are the same. For love to enrich your relationship, it needs firm foundations and a solid ground. It is through the foundations of the relationship we meet our needs. Love then enriches the bond that already exists. You could argue, without foundations such as respect, honesty, trust, and equality, it isn't really love, but attachment.

In abusive relationships, there is a dependency on the abuser to meet all your needs. This gives them power to withhold your needs as part of the abuse, causing you harm. In healthy relationships, we are not reliant on one person to meet all of our needs, nor is it their responsibility. We have a responsibility to meet our own needs, and we do this through learning to self-soothe, prioritise ourselves, set boundaries, and building a network of connections. This means there is consistency to having our needs met, as there is more than one relationship providing us with safety, including the one we have with ourselves.

Meeting your needs in healthy relationships looks like:

Getting to know and accept your needs!

This is a fundamental step in meeting your needs. When you feel triggered, reflect on what feeling triggered you. Did you feel unseen, powerless, judged, uncared for, trapped? These signal unmet needs in past relationships. Or when you feel over responsible, overextend yourself, or don't uphold a boundary, ask yourself, what needs of my own did I forgo? These are suppressed needs to attend to. Give them space and accept they are valid. Conversely, when you feel contented, what needs are being met? This helps you identify which needs to cultivate in your relationships to feel happy and secure.

Communicating your needs!

Although it sounds simple, it's challenging to communicate your needs if this was previously met with abuse.

We shy away from communicating our needs if we struggle to accept that they are valid, and we fear others will react unfavourably. We might also be prone to assuming our relationship needs should be obvious. It should be obvious we need affection, connection and warmth! But people can't mind read. How they show their affection and the level they show may differ from how you need it to be shown. Communication is key to having your needs met.

To meet your own needs, check in with yourself regularly. How are you feeling? Are you giving yourself enough rest? Are you showing yourself compassion? This gives you autonomy over having your needs met and enables you to make choices to take care of your wellbeing.

Healthy boundaries!

Healthy boundaries create safety in your environment and relationships. They also facilitate authentic connection. You cannot connect authentically when you forgo your own needs to accommodate others. Give yourself time to pause and reflect. Ask yourself whether saying yes will impact negatively on your wellbeing. Learning to say no is a major step in prioritising and recognising your needs are valid.

For healthy boundaries with yourself, reflect on how your environment affects your mood. Do you have healthy boundaries around content you consume, such as what news stories you read or social media accounts you follow? If you notice certain accounts negatively affect your wellbeing, unfollow them. This is a boundary with yourself that supports you in meeting your own needs and creating safety. You can reflect on how you spend your time, financial boundaries, relationships, self-care routines, exercise, self-talk, and coping mechanisms, such as mindfulness and breathing exercises.

Healthy Relationships

Many survivors find a healthy relationship after abuse the hardest relationship to be in... *initially*. It is hard to allow yourself to be vulnerable, to discern between triggers and intuition, and to believe you are worthy of love. You still feel on high alert and haven't made new experiences to build evidence that people are trustworthy. There is also a lack of self-trust and awareness of how to function in a healthy dynamic when you have been surviving in an abusive one. These are key issues. We don't want to commit to another abuser and get hurt again. Equally, we don't want to close ourselves off from safe, fulfilling relationships.

Discernment or Triggers?

A major point of confusion is whether the unease in new relationships is discernment or being triggered. This is because of feeling disconnected from your intuition and your heightened survival responses. Survivors often express doubt about how they read a situation, whether their new partner is behaving reasonably and whether their own emotional reactions are acceptable. They ask questions like, 'is it fair of me to expect them to spend more time with me or am I being controlling?' or, 'they said they don't want to share certain things with me, and I need to respect their privacy, but it feels like they're hiding something.' They are afraid to raise any issues or take action, because of their doubts over whether the situation is ok, unreasonable, abusive or they are feeling triggered from the past.

Triggers

Triggers feel reactive because they are centred on survival and protection. They derive from our primitive brain and have a direct connection with our body. Emotions and physical symptoms can feel intense. As the primitive brain takes over, it temporarily shuts down the higher brain, which is your conscious mind, and therefore you may feel overwhelmed, have racing thoughts and feel a loss of your senses or a loss of control.

Discernment

Discernment feels responsive rather than reactive because it is centred on perception and judgement. As it derives from our awareness and consciousness, we often feel calm and mindful, with an objective outlook of the situation. Emotions and physical responses are present but less intense than when triggered. Thoughts are also clearer, although they can be clouded by self-doubt and uncertainty.

Sometimes harmless stimuli trigger us, such as innocent words, actions or places, which trigger a response from a past negative experience. Other times, however, when we experience doubt about our response, it is because of one of two things.

First, our response is discernment, but we don't trust our own judgement. We are not comfortable with the situation, and the other person's behaviour crosses our relationship boundaries. Or it may be *neither person is in the wrong*. You hold different perspectives, both of which are reasonable, and you have discerned there is a point of conflict to resolve. However, previous experiences of covert abuse and gaslighting mean you doubt your ability to perceive interactions reasonably.

We doubt whether our perspective is fair and whether it is worthy of being considered.

Your perspective is important and deserves consideration.

Second is, we experience discernment and feeling triggered simultaneously. There is a situation we have discerned is not ok, and it has triggered a disproportionate response in our survival system. We then doubt not only our ability to perceive interactions reasonably, but also our intense emotional, physical, and psychological reaction to it. This can lead to us invalidating our feelings and judgement as we attribute them solely to being triggered.

Recognising you are exhibiting an ability to discern right from wrong, your personal boundaries and what you are comfortable with in your relationships helps you to build self-trust. Your responses shouldn't be dismissed as past trauma. Instead, reflect on *how you have responded.* How intense was your response? What was the situation and what emotions were strongest? If you felt ignored, for example, and this triggered a fear of emotional neglect and abandonment, the interactions which led to you feeling ignored still need to be addressed. Communicating how you felt *and why* will help to create safety in healthy relationships. It disperses miscommunication and allows others to take responsibility for their behaviour. This, in turn, provides the opportunity for conflict resolution and mutual understanding of how to approach similar situations in the future. Where you were triggered by a reasonable interaction, it allows for you to honour your response, to feel understood in your relationship and be given reassurance.

HEALED TO BE LOVED?

We hear a lot about self-love. The thing is, when self-esteem is incredibly low, self-love feels out of reach. We learn to love ourselves in the present by extending our love to the parts of self that were unloved in the past. Yet, it's a heavy task to love parts of ourselves we feel are deeply unlovable. There will be days where you can be your biggest cheerleader, and on other days, accepting how you feel is the kindest act of self-love.

After abuse, you don't have to be healed to love and receive love. This is harmful for survivors to believe. It's another narrative that says you aren't worthy of love as you are and blames you for not having the relationships you hope for. Whilst some of us find safety and peace in solitude, for others this belief prevents us from seeking connection, when in fact, receiving love is restorative. When we experience genuine and healthy relationships, it is an example we are worthy of love, and we are worthy of our own love. *You don't need to rush into romantic love.* We heal through building connections that are safe, genuine, and accepting. Positive connection also helps to regulate your nervous system, which supports you to feel safe in your environment.

RECOGNISING LOVE

When we have experienced hurtful or abusive relationships, we look to soothe the wounds by finding a relationship that will never disappoint us, never hurt us, and we never feel the same way again. In our quest to avoid harm, we are drawn to the promises and beautiful appearance of idealisation. We become more susceptible to love bombing and the falsehoods of the abuser's persona. It's the classic, 'if it seems too good to be true, it probably is', yet because we know the pain of a harmful relationship, we don't want to risk anything less than perfect.

In letting go of striving for the perfect relationship, we become less vulnerable to abuse.

Becoming aware of how abuse was present in your past helps you to recognise what is and isn't loving behaviour in relationships. The beauty is, love is not a fixed construct. You have the autonomy to define love however you choose to, and to prioritise the values important *to you*. You can build relationships with people who share these values, rather than the abuser, who takes advantage of them.

Consistency in Love

Psychologist John Gottman, who has extensively researched relationships, found couples in healthy relationships have five positive interactions for every negative interaction during conflict. This was coined the magic ratio 5:1 and deemed optimal for maintaining satisfying relationships. *Even in disagreement*, attempts to interact positively outweigh negative communication. These include attentiveness, affection, appreciation, a sincere apology and empathy. Outside of conflict, healthy couples have an even higher positive to negative ratio of 20:1.

The magic ratio can be applied to any relationship, not just married couples, and shows a healthy relationship isn't one without conflict (or idealised), but good enough. There is consistency in positive interactions, and this provides the opportunity for realistic expectations, reparative communication, and mutual growth.

Whilst I'm not suggesting you should permit abuse if it is counterbalanced with five positive interactions, it does help us to gauge a healthy level of relationship conflict. *And to consider how we communicate during conflict.* Often after abuse, we question whether allowing any negative interactions is once again tolerating abuse.

Although it doesn't mean everything less than this ratio signals abuse, you can ask yourself how often the abuser met your needs? What ratio of positive to negative interactions did you have with them overall? How did they interact during conflict?

Holding this in mind provides an opportunity to gain clarity.

When you navigate new relationships and you are building trust in yourself and others, this is a helpful tool to gauge whether your relationship is healthy, and to maintain relationship satisfaction through aiming for a good balance.

Principles of Love

Self-reflecting on the values important to you in a loving relationship supports you in keeping your values a part of it. When you are aware of how you would like to love and be loved, it empowers you to take steps towards building this connection. These include principles such as respect, empathy, safety, validation, connection, and authenticity. Having clarity of your principles not only supports you in maintaining healthy relationships but helps to protect you from the gradual shifts towards harmful behaviour in abusive relationships. By holding greater awareness, you recognise sooner when the relationship deviates from the principles of love that matter to you most.

Love is Action

We express love through action. This isn't grandiose displays of love or compensating for extreme lows with extreme highs, it's showing love through everyday interactions. It is showing love through consistency. When loving words are supported by respectful, reliable, trustworthy, and empathetic actions, the relationship becomes one that is nurturing and feels safe. *And where love is felt.*

It is through small gestures, such as showing compassion, giving a hug, or dedicating time, we feel most loved. It is the culmination of these small but significant actions which convey the presence of love. Conversely, controlling actions feel least loving as they prevent authentic connection. We can see how the abusive relationship is starved of love, with a lack of loving gestures and an excess of control. If they say they love you, but their actions are controlling, you will not feel loved. You are going to feel starved of it.

To cultivate feeling love in healthy relationships, it's important to communicate how you express and receive love. Reflect on when you felt most loved, or in what situations you would feel loved, and what actions you associate with showing love to others. People express and receive love differently, so communicating which small gestures are impactful enables you to create a greater presence of love in your relationships.

The bottom line is, in a healthy relationship you shouldn't have to think five steps ahead, walk on eggshells, anticipate their mood, take blame for all tensions, read their mind, apologise for their behaviour and fear they may stop loving you from one day to the next. This isn't healthy love; it is control. You deserve a love that is enriching, stable, and authentic. One where love is felt, not uttered to excuse abusive behaviour. You deserve to be happy, and you need to feel safe. Most of all, you deserve to be loved as you are.

5 conflict repair attempts in healthy relationships:

- o Attempting to understand one another's perspective.
- o Owning up to mistakes, genuinely apologising, and each recognising their role in the dispute.
- o Taking breaks from discussing the issue when someone feels emotionally overwhelmed, conflict becomes heated, or attempts to resolve become circular.
- o Showing compassion for one another's emotional responses.
- o Communicating how you feel to reduce miscommunication.

SURVIVOR'S GUIDE
BREAKING THE CHAINS TAKEAWAYS:

· Ruminating on how much you've invested in the abuser is an attempt to avoid feelings of shame, regret and loss. When we stop viewing endings as failures, actively choose to invest in ourselves, and introduce small joys so loss does not define our lives, we enable ourselves to work through these feelings.

· Believing in the abuser's goodness does not change the reality of living with abuse. Reflecting on your attitudes towards romance, and whether you romanticise relationships, helps you identify whether you are drawn to believe in the good, counter to their unhealthy behaviours, and to set boundaries.

· The question, 'what if they change', comes from underlying fears of whether you gave up too soon, if you caused the abuse or if you could have had the relationship you hoped for. Coming to terms with these fears will support you in letting go of the fear of them changing.

· Abusers aren't always abusive because it doesn't serve them to abuse everyone. It does not minimise their abusive behaviour towards you, and it is not a reflection of your worth; it is a protection of their image.

· If unhealthy relationships are all you've known, then healthy love can leave you feeling exposed, smothered and uncomfortable. Redefining love is empowering because it is acknowledging you don't have to accept relationships that hurt you.

· The belief 'love hurts' normalises abusive behaviour. Redefine love as safe, where your emotional vulnerability is treated with care.

· Unconditional love can lead to unconditional tolerance. Loving relationships include boundaries. This is not only loving to yourself but towards others as it helps maintain healthy connections.

· Love is not all you need. You have other relationship needs that are valid. To meet these needs yourself and in your relationships, acknowledge and accept them, communicate them, and set healthy boundaries.

· Healthy relationships are not perfect but positive interactions far outweigh the negative. Love is shown through actions and there is consistency in upholding relationship values and principles. You deserve a relationship where love is felt, not uttered to excuse abuse.

Breaking the Chains Journal Prompt

In my relationships I value...

These principles are important to me...

I feel most loved when...

Afterword:

End Credits Scene

One difficulty of writing a book about emotional and psychological abuse is that many behaviours are not exclusive to abusive relationships. For example, not everyone who criticises you is an abuser, yet highly critical behaviour is often a staple pattern of emotional abuse.

This is one of the ongoing issues with maintaining clarity in your experiences and confidence in your perception. We are constantly told not to judge too harshly, and everyone has toxic behaviours. These words flare up our inner panic and shake our sense of peace. How then do I discuss these behaviours, conveying the significance of the abuse and its impact, without the risk of appearing to label anyone who shows unhealthy behaviour as an abuser? How to put it into words, so if the behaviour resonates with survivors, they don't label themselves an abuser?

This was an ongoing thought in my mind throughout writing this book. To validate the experience of abuse and capture the severity of it, without giving the feeling that everyday human behaviours are being labelled abusive. The importance of not having others dismiss the survivors' experience, again, yet not causing further confusion over their own behaviour and other relationships.

I know learning about abuse triggers feelings of shame, and I want to encourage you to approach this feeling with curiosity, not fear. Understanding what triggers shame helps to heal the wound. When you are afraid of shame you will try to avoid it, but you cannot shift it unless you face and disarm it.

When you look at your experiences in hindsight, don't judge yourself according to the understanding you hold now. We often expect ourselves to handle abuse in the same way as healthy relationship conflicts and breakups. This might literally not have been possible with the limited freedom you had in the abusive relationship. You cannot hold yourself to the same expectations. You can, however, show yourself the grace of compassion.

Let me end by going back to the foreign language film. Well, I like to think this film has an end credits scene. End credits scenes are often dedicated to one character in the film, and it shows us their story isn't over. In fact, it tells us their story is worth telling. Their worth isn't defined by how another's story impacted their lives. *They were born worthy.* And the most transformative, beautiful, and defining part of their story hasn't been told.

And the character in this end credits scene is you.

Notes

The Three A's

Awareness

Emotional & Psychological Abuse: An abuser by definition is…: (2008). *Cambridge advanced learner's dictionary.* Cambridge, Cambridge University Press.

Micro Patterns: In his book, Why Does He Do That?, Lundy Bancroft profiles this type of abuse: BANCROFT, L. (2003). *Why does he do that.* New York, NY, Berkley.

Power and Control: In her book Power and Control, Sandra Horley discusses: HORLEY, S. (2018). *Power and Control: Why Charming Men Can Make Dangerous Lovers.* Random House.

Coercive Control: Women's Aid, a leading UK charity: Women's Aid (N.D) *What is Coercive Control?* Women's Aid, viewed 02 Feb 2022, <https://www.womensaid.org.uk/information-support/what-is-domestic-abuse/coercive-control/>

Acknowledgement

Evil Intention?: Psychopaths are aware of moral choices: PLETTI C, LOTTO L, BUODO G, & SARLO M. (2017). It's immoral, but I'd do it! Psychopathy traits affect decision-making in sacrificial dilemmas and in everyday moral situations. *British Journal of Psychology (London, England : 1953).* 108, 351-368.

Gender Stereotypes: One study found men who grew up with family or friends: REITZEL-JAFFE, D., AND DAVID A. WOLFE. (2001). Predictors of relationship abuse among young men. *Violence & Abuse Abstracts.* 7, 163-252.

Are Abusers Angry?: One study into abusive men found they were driven by a social need to control: GONDOLF, E. W. (1989). *The case against anger control treatment programs for batterers.* Ottawa, Dept. of National Health and Welfare.

Are Abusers Angry?: The Freedom Programme supports this theory: CRAVEN, P. (2008). *Living with the dominator: a book about the Freedom Programme.* Kinighton, Freedom Programme.

Acceptance

Long-Term Effects: Long-term effects of emotional abuse include depression: Healthline (16 May 2018) *What Are the Short- and Long- Term Effects of Emotional Abuse?,* Healthline, viewed 04 Oct 2021 <https://www.healthline.com/health/mental-health/effects-of-emotional-abuse>

Untangling Self

I am going to adapt the Cycle of Abuse: WALKER, L. E. (2009). *The battered woman syndrome.* New York, NY, Springer Pub. Co. http://site.ebrary.com/id/10286258.

The Power and Control Wheel is another great resource: Domestic Abuse Intervention Programs (2017), *Wheel Information Center: Understanding the Power and Control Wheel,* Domestic Abuse Intervention Programs, Home of the Duluth Model, viewed 06 Oct 2021, <https://www.theduluthmodel.org/wheels/>

Building Tension

Low Self-Esteem: A siege is defined as…: (2008). *Cambridge advanced learner's dictionary.* Cambridge, Cambridge University Press.

Low Self-Esteem: Our sense of self-worth is deeply affected, which can harm our mental health: NHS (06 Feb 2020), *Raising Low Self-Esteem,* NHS, viewed 11 Oct 2021, <https://www.nhs.uk/mental-health/self-help/tips-and-support/raise-low-self-esteem/>

Acute Pressure

Neglectful Behaviour: Research shows it activates the same parts of the brain as physical pain: WILLIAMS, K. D., & NIDA, S. A. (2011). Ostracism: Consequences and Coping. *Current Directions in Psychological Science.* 20, 71-75.

Survival Mode: Fight: The fight response is an attempt to protect yourself…: Healthline (2021) *The Beginner's Guide to Trauma Responses,* Healthline, viewed 17 Oct 2021, <https://www.healthline.com/health/mental-health/fight-flight-freeze-fawn>

Survival Mode: Bessel Van Der Kolk discusses in his book, The Body Keeps the Score: KOLK, B. A. V. D. (2015). *The body keeps the score: mind, brain and body in the transformation of trauma.* Penguin.

Reactive Abuse: Psychotherapist Pete Walker describes how being trapped in the fight response: Walker. P. (N.D). *The 4Fs: A Trauma Typology in Complex PTSD,* Pete Walker, viewed 07 Feb 2022, <http://petewalker.com/fourFs_TraumaTypologyComplexPTSD.htm>

Stress Toll: Stress is a known contributor and aggravator to various health issues: American Psychological Association. (2013). *How Stress Affects Your Health,* APA, viewed 03 Feb 2022, <https://www.apa.org/topics/stress/health>

Manipulation

Fake Emotions: Research suggests they are in control of their anger: GONDOLF, E. W. (1989). *The case against anger control treatment programs for batterers.* Ottawa, Dept. of National Health and Welfare.

Trauma Bonding

Trauma Bonding Behaviours: There tends to be two main characteristics to a trauma bonded relationship: *Logan, M. H. (2018). Stockholm Syndrome: Held Hostage by the One You Love. Violence and Gender,5(2), 67-69. doi:10.1089/vio.2017.0076*

An Addictive Bond: Hormones also contribute to the strength of the trauma bond: Raypole, C. (2020). *How to Recognize and Break Traumatic Bonds,* Healthline, viewed 27 Oct 2021, <https://www.healthline.com/health/mental-health/trauma-bonding>

Potential versus Reality

Research shows it takes just a tenth of a second to form an impression of someone: WILLIS, J., & TODOROV, A. (2006). First Impressions: Making up Your Mind after a 100-Ms Exposure to a Face. *Psychological Science.* 17, 592-598.

The Potential

Mirroring: One research study associated higher levels of narcissistic traits with higher levels of identity instability: DI PIERRO R., DI SARNO M., PRETI E., MADEDDU F., & DI MATTEI V.E. (2018). The role of identity instability in the relationship between narcissism and emotional empathy. *Psychoanalytic Psychology.* 35, 237-243.

The Reality

They are also a part of normal childhood development: Satow. R. (2017). *Idealization and Contempt,* Psychology Today, viewed 07 Nov 202, <https://www.psychologytoday.com/gb/blog/life-after-50/201702/idealization-and-contempt>

Reconciling Dissonance

For the Abuser: In the book, Group Work with Populations at Risk, Steven Stosny discusses: Stosny, S. cited in GREIF, G. L., & KNIGHT, C. (2017). *Group work with populations at risk.* Oxford University Press

For the Survivor: According to Maslow's hierarchy of needs: Maslow, A.H. (1943). *"A Theory of Human Motivation".* In Psychological Review, 50 (4), 430-437.

Stoking the Belief: Further to this, abusers with fragile high self-esteem, such as highly narcissistic, have a sense of superiority: Rose, S. (2019) *Do Narcissists Have Low Self-Esteem.* Steve Rose PHD Counselling, viewed 27 Nov 2021, <https://steverosephd.com/do-narcissists-have-low-self-esteem>

Breaking the Chains

On average, it takes a woman seven attempts: VPWF (2022). *Why it takes women 7 attempts to leave an abusive relationship – and how you can help.* Virginia Physicians for Women, viewed

08 Jan 2022, <https://vpfw.com/blog/why-it-takes-women-7-attempts-to-leave-an-abusive-relationship/>

Alternatively, lesbian and bisexual women are less likely to come forward about intimate partner abuse: CHESLEY, L. C., MACAULAY, D., & RISTOCK, J. L. (1998). *Abuse in lesbian relationships: information and resources.* [Ottawa], Health Canada.

Deconstructing Thoughts

Sunk Cost Fallacy: In her book, The Highly Sensitive Person's Guide to Dealing with Toxic People, Shahida Arabi explains: ARABI, S. (2020). *Highly Sensitive Person's Guide to Dealing with Toxic People: How to Reclaim Your Power from Narcissists and Other Manipulators.* New Harbinger Publications.

Deconstructing: I've Invested so Much: In her book Modern Families: Parents and Children in New Family Forms, Susan Golombok discusses: Golombok, S. (2015). *Modern families: Parents and children in new family forms.* Cambridge University Press.

Acknowledgement: It is notoriously difficult for abusers to change: Stosny, S. (2005). *Group Treatment of Intimate Partner Abusers. In G. L. Greif & P. H. Ephross (Eds.), Group work with populations at risk (pp. 226–237).* Oxford University Press.

Redefining Love

Reframe: Love with Boundaries: Of the four parenting styles: Baumrind, D. (1991). *Parenting styles and adolescent development.* In J. Brooks-Gunn, R. M. Lerner, & A. C. Petersen

(Eds.), The encyclopaedia on adolescence (pp. 746-758). New York: Garland Publishing.

Reframe: Love with Boundaries: In her book Set Boundaries, Find Peace, Nedra Glover Tawwab discusses: TAWWAB, N. G. (2021). *Set boundaries, find peace: a guide to reclaiming yourself.* Piatkus.

Discernment or Triggers?: They derive from our primitive brain: KOLK, B. A. V. D. (2015). *The body keeps the score: mind, brain and body in the transformation of trauma.* Penguin.

Recognising Love: Psychologist John Gottman, who has extensively researched relationships: Benson, K. (2017). *The Magic Relationship Ratio, According to Science.* The Gottman Institute, viewed 07 Feb 2022, <https://www.gottman.com/blog/the-magic-relationship-ratio-according-science/>

Recognising Love: It's through small gestures, such as showing compassion: Bohn, K. (2017). *Love actually: Americans agree on what makes people 'feel the love'.* PennState, viewed 17 Jun 2022, <https://www.psu.edu/news/research/story/love-actually-americans-agree-what-makes-people-feel-love/>

ABOUT THE AUTHOR

Emma founded The Personal Growth Project in 2017 to support the growth of survivors of emotional and psychological abuse, through her writing and mentoring. She has established a large online community, and her social media posts have become a source of providing clarity. Her gift is to put into words an experience that is often hard to describe.

Emma's background is working with young people who have experienced abuse, to help them recognise healthy and unhealthy bonds in their relationships, and to help them gain confidence and clarity. Emma has since studied Counselling and will complete her Psychology degree in 2023. She trained in integrative therapeutic counselling, combining person-centered, psychodynamic and CBT methods. She has in-depth knowledge of the experiences of abuse which has been gained through attending courses, first person accounts, self-teaching and personal experience.

Made in the USA
Middletown, DE
15 August 2023